CW00688765

ARMY CADET YEARBOOK

ARMY CADET YEARBOOK

Army Cadets' commissioning editors: Jack Cavilla, Joanna Simpson

Editor: Rosanna Rothery

Editorial team: Kathryn Lewis, Abi Manning,
Melissa Morris, Arwen Moses, Jo Rees, Selena Young

Lead designer: Dale Stiling

Designer: Gemma Richards

Production: Tamsin Powell

Cover image: Cadet Corporal Revelo, taken by PI Doug Stuart.

www.armycadets.com

ISBN 978-1-9160859-5-4

First published in Great Britain in 2021 by Army Cadets UK

Text © Crown Copyright - Army Cadets 2021

Design and layout © Crown Copyright - Army Cadets 2021

Printed in Great Britain

www.saltmedia.co.uk

01271 859299   ideas@saltmedia.co.uk

MIX
Paper from
responsible sources
FSC® C010353

ARMY CADET
YEARBOOK
YEARBOOK
Issue 2

Photos: Kate Knight

Welcome

I'm excited to welcome you to the second issue of the annual *Army Cadet Yearbook*. It provides a moment to read and reflect on some of the remarkable achievements across the detachments during the past twelve months.

I would like to thank all those who 'kept the flame alive' by providing virtual support and training during national and regional lockdowns. The response from cadets and CFAVs to the Covid-19 pandemic has been truly incredible and is reflected in the uplifting news stories featured in this book.

Despite the various challenges, I was pleased so many cadets and CFAVs were able to gather for the highlight of the year: summer camps. Our ten-page feature captures the spirit of fun, friendship and belonging, as well as the action and adventure enjoyed across all regions of the UK.

Within this Yearbook you'll also find interviews with inspirational adventurers such as TV presenter Bear Grylls and round-the-world sailor Tracy Edwards. You'll get the opportunity to test your skills and survival knowledge, and learn more about the new Army Cadets Syllabus. You'll also discover sports you may not have tried before, learn how to navigate by the stars, and meet former cadets who've gone on to achieve amazing things.

Read on to discover how Army Cadets promotes fun, friendship, action, adventure and selfless service, plus incredible opportunities to skill up and learn new things. Our purpose is to set people up for lifelong success.

In April this year, we received the very sad news that HRH The Prince Philip, Duke of Edinburgh, had died. As our Colonel-in-Chief for 68 years, Prince Philip inspired generations of cadets and volunteers, so with great pride we present a six-page tribute to an exceptional man who provided tireless service to Army Cadets.

Enjoy the Yearbook – and don't forget 'To Inspire To Achieve'.

Brigadier Stuart Williams OBE
Deputy Commander Cadets

» A word from Commander Cadets

What a year it has been! The global pandemic has been a challenge for all, yet despite this I've been blown away by the achievements and commitment of cadets and adult volunteers during the past 12 months.

Although I haven't been able to see as much of the organisation this year as I'd have wished to, what I have been fortunate to witness has been outstanding. The activity that's taken place, both virtual and face to face, has been first class – clearly everyone was eager to get back to it.

There have been some important lessons learnt through the experience of the last year. We need to build on them by innovating where we can, striving to make this fantastic organisation the best it can be and delivering the ultimate Army Cadets experience for all.

This is another fantastic issue of the Yearbook with great features and articles. Enjoy!

Major General David Eastman MBE
Commander Cadets

Contents

Contents

114

118

192

The briefing
ARMY CADETS 101

Army Cadets National Ambassador Jordan Wylie calls Army Cadets 'the nation's best kept secret', so what is the organisation all about, and what are our values?

Photo: Kate Knight

The Army Cadet Force is a national voluntary youth organisation, sponsored by the Army to provide challenging military, adventurous and community activities.

Its aim is to inspire young people to achieve success in life with a spirit of service to the Queen, their country and their local community, and to help them become good citizens. This is achieved by:

❯ Providing progressive cadet training, often of a challenging and exciting nature, to foster confidence, self-reliance, initiative, loyalty and a sense of service to other people.

❯ Encouraging the development of personal powers of practical leadership and the ability to work successfully as a member of a team.

❯ Stimulating an interest in the Army, its achievements, skills and values.

❯ Advising and preparing those considering a career in the Services, or with the Reserve Forces.

To Inspire To Achieve

Army Cadets values

>> COURAGE

Courage is both physical and moral. Physical courage is what lets us motivate others when the activity or the environment is hard or demanding, such as hiking across Dartmoor as part of a Ten Tors team. Moral courage is having the strength and confidence to do what is right even when it might make us unpopular, such as standing up to bullying. It is also the courage to insist on maintaining the highest standards of behaviour. Both physical and moral courage are equally important, and showing courage in all forms earns us respect and fosters trust.

>> DISCIPLINE

Discipline helps us all to work effectively as part of a team. It isn't just about being told off for doing something wrong; it's about having the self-control to not do the wrong thing, and self-confidence to stand up to those who do.

Self-discipline is the ability to make the time to polish our boots, iron our uniform and be smart on parade, no matter what other distractions are around us.

Discipline helps build our team so everyone is trusted to do the task well. Good discipline means we all do the right thing – even when things get difficult.

>> RESPECT FOR OTHERS

Respect for others means we treat others as we'd like to be treated.

Army Cadets is a very varied and mixed team, and we must not discriminate against anyone because of their gender or because they have a different ethnic background, religion or sexual orientation to us.

We recognise the value everyone brings to the team and that they all have different viewpoints and ways to contribute. We have respect for others, not only because it is a legal obligation, but because teams that embrace difference and diversity are stronger.

>> LOYALTY

Loyalty is what keeps teams together. In Army Cadets that team could be our detachment, county, section, contingent or any other team we are part of, such as on an expedition, overseas exchange or sports team.

When we work together in a team we achieve so much more. However, loyalty must only support positive behaviours and actions. Loyalty to a team should never allow poor behaviours or the wrong thing to be done. Letting others stray from our values is not loyal to the team.

>> INTEGRITY

Integrity means being truthful and honest, and trusting those above us in the organisation.

When we show integrity we build trust in ourselves and in our team, and this makes the team stronger and able to do more.

Showing integrity also helps others outside Army Cadets trust us and helps us to do more in our communities. It's important that everyone, from the newest cadet to senior officers, demonstrates integrity in everything they do, otherwise trust will be eroded.

>> SELFLESS COMMITMENT

Selfless commitment is critical to good leadership and teamwork. It is about putting the needs of others ahead of our own to help everyone succeed.

We demonstrate this when we help someone with a lesson they are finding difficult, rather than going off for a break, or when we hang back with someone who is struggling on an expedition, rather than speeding on ahead. Without selfless commitment we can't be good leaders. Remember the motto of Royal Military Academy Sandhurst, where Army officers are trained, is 'Serve to Lead'.

Lorraine Kelly

After the restrictions and difficulties that lockdown placed on cadets and CFAVs, Lorraine shares a message of inspiration and enthusiasm for the year ahead.

As Army Cadets' National Honorary Colonel I am so proud of the young people who join the Cadets and make such a difference through their selfless commitment.

Looking through the pages of the second annual Yearbook it's fantastic to read about cadets going above and beyond to serve those in need in their community, respond to emergencies with first-aid skills and raise impressive sums of money for worthy causes. These inspiring stories are just the tip of the iceberg as I know that, across the detachments, young people are out there showing determination, community spirit and generosity.

When asked about Army Cadets, I always stress that the cadet movement is for *all* young people, not just those who have ambitions to join the armed forces. Whatever their talents or passions, the kind of opportunities and skills featured within the following pages will set them up for life – no matter what they eventually do.

'I always stress that the cadet movement is for all young people, not just those who have ambitions to join the armed forces'

Whether you're musical, relish outdoor adventures, have a gift for understanding technology, show flair for fieldcraft, excel at sport, take pride in drill or love to cook, you'll find the Yearbook is packed with ideas and inspiration.

Being in the Cadets is about making new friends, gaining confidence, teamwork, inclusion and celebrating our differences and strengths; together we are a powerful force.

Finally, an enormous thank you to our Cadet Force Adult Volunteers who put in so much time and effort to make it all happen – your energy, enthusiasm and passion is astonishing!

Lorraine Kelly CBE
Army Cadets' National Honorary Colonel

Lorraine as Honorary Black Watch Colonel in 2009, inspecting officer duties at the Royal Gun salute to mark HRH The Queen's birthday at Stirling Castle in Scotland

Photo: Danny Lawson

Meet the
AMBASSADORS

We've got four inspirational figures who spread the word about Army Cadets and what we do. Here's your need-to-know.

Sally Orange

Army Cadets Ambassador Sally is an endurance runner, adventurer, mental health champion and multiple Guinness World Records™ title holder.

In addition to having run over 50 marathons on every continent in the world, Sally had a distinguished 22-year military career in the Royal Army Medical Corps as a physiotherapy officer.

She also captained the first British female team to complete the world's toughest cycle race – the Race Across America – and has cycled the length of New Zealand, swum the English Channel relay, completed eight Ironman triathlons, climbed numerous 6,000m+ mountains, and skied 250km across the largest plateau in the Arctic Circle, raising thousands of pounds for charity.

Sally has also publicly shared her experience of suffering from severe depression and chronic anxiety – read more about her activities to raise awareness of these issues on page 100.

Photo: Kate Knight

To Inspire To Achieve

Photo: Kate Knight

Photo: A360DEGREES

Jordan Wylie

Army Cadets Ambassador Jordan is a former soldier, extreme adventurer and one of the stars of Channel 4's BAFTA-nominated shows *Hunted* and *Celebrity Hunted*.

He served for a decade in the British Army where he specialised in military intelligence, reconnaissance and surveillance operations.

Jordan is also the bestselling author of *Citadel: The True Story of One Man's War Against the Pirates of Somalia*, and has undertaken numerous major charity expeditions including Running Dangerously and Barefoot Warrior which involved climbing Mount Kilimanjaro barefoot. He also campaigns to reduce the stigma around mental illness.

Jordan's recently been filming a new documentary about Army Cadets. Read all about it on page 192.

Craig Mathieson

Polar explorer Craig has been involved in numerous expeditions to the Antarctic and Arctic.

He led the first dedicated Scottish expedition to the South Pole in 2004, skied to the North Pole in 2006, was appointed Explorer-in-Residence by Royal Scottish Geographical Society in 2013 and recently became membership director of the Great Britain and Ireland Chapter of The Explorers Club.

Craig also runs The Polar Academy, a project that takes young people in Scotland on challenging and confidence-building expeditions to the Arctic.

In 2021, as a result of the pandemic, he took a team of young people on quite a different expedition altogether. Turn to page 42 to find out what happened.

Photo: Kate Knight

'Big Phil' Campion

Army Cadets Champion Phil is a former soldier, author and TV personality. Phil's Army career saw him join the Royal Hampshire Regiment at age 16 before passing his Commando course, P Company and Special Forces selection. His career took him on operational service to Northern Ireland, West Africa and the Balkans, among other parts of the world.

He's published four very successful books and starred in his own TV documentary *Big Phil's War*. Phil's work has helped raise the profile and funds of numerous charities, in keeping with his aim of putting as much into life as he's taken out.

Turn to page 40 to find out about one of Phil's recent adventures.

HRH The Prince Philip
Duke of Edinburgh

1921-2021

Photo: Michael Nolan

To Inspire To Achieve

I t was with great sadness that we received the news that our Colonel-in-Chief had died on 9 April 2021. He held the appointment from 1953 until his death, and inspired generations of cadets, volunteers and staff. We're proud to shine a spotlight on his tireless work and pay tribute to a remarkable man.

Major General David Eastman MBE, Commander Cadets

'HRH The Prince Philip, Duke of Edinburgh, had a longstanding and very special relationship with the ACF dating back to January 1953, when he was appointed Colonel-in-Chief by HM The Queen. That he held this appointment for the rest of his life is testament to his significant commitment to our young people and to the ACF as an organisation.

'The ACF was honoured to be one of the first organisations to pilot the Duke of Edinburgh's Award (DofE) in 1956 and the first to deliver the Colonel-in-Chief's vision of enabling young people to realise their potential. Since then, tens of thousands of cadets have achieved an award and benefitted from his foresight and vision.

'In all of the Colonel-in-Chief's engagements with the ACF (the last of which was a visit to the Cadet Training Centre Frimley Park on 17 October 2008 to mark the 50th anniversary of its foundation), cadets and adult volunteers who met him were always hugely impressed by his keen interest in, and knowledge of, the ACF.

'Our Colonel-in-Chief felt passionately about improving the lives of young people. He will be sadly missed by all associated with the ACF, both past and present, and we consider ourselves extremely fortunate to have benefitted from his enduring commitment for so long.'

Colonel Clint Riley OBE, ACF – Army Cadet Force Colonel Cadets

'HRH The Duke of Edinburgh gave a life of service to our sovereign, our nation and the Commonwealth, and the impact he had on us as members of the ACF was impressive. We are all the better for his interest.

'Those who met him were always extremely impressed by his keen and knowledgeable interest. He genuinely wanted to know how the ACF was doing and generously made an annual donation – the last received in January 2021. Whenever he visited, he had time for everyone and engaged all with his sharp wit and knowledge of the Cadets.

'A lot of people have their own stories of meeting the Duke but I met him at St James's Palace at a DofE Gold Award ceremony. It was fantastic to engage with him and talk about what our cadets were doing. For the cadets receiving awards it was a wonderful experience but he also turned to the parents and chatted to them. It was so special; everyone left feeling six feet tall.

'He has been an inspiration to us for 68 years and will continue to be, as his legacy continues with the DofE Award. We have lost the Duke as our Colonel-in-Chief but his Award will continue to give our cadets a great start in life.'

Photo: Mike Smith / MOD

Presentation of the Banner, 2005

HRH The Duke of Edinburgh presented three personal Banners to the ACF. Two (presented in 1960 and 1982) are laid up in St Peter's Church in Frimley. The latest Banner, presented in 2005, is held at the Cadet Training Centre Frimley Park.

Prior to the 2005 presentation (shown here in pictures) at Royal Military Academy Sandhurst, he took the trouble to find out exactly how the event would be organised and even chose the two hymns (*To Be A Pilgrim* and *I Vow To Thee My Country*). After the presentation he stayed on for tea where he took the trouble to speak to every single cadet and adult volunteer who was there representing the ACF counties, battalions and sectors throughout the UK.

Photo: Peter Dance / Tempest Photography

Centenary Parade, 1960

Lieutenant Colonel (retd) Mike Gerrish, MBE (pictured), remembers being chosen to carry the banner for 2nd Battalion, Northumberland ACF during its 1960 presentation at the ACF's centenary. The parade took place in Tynemouth and the guest of honour was Major General Lord Thurlow.

'It was a fine occasion, and a very proud moment for me,' he said.

Despite his mother taking photos of his involvement, a fault with her camera meant he only has a few pictures of the day (including the image below) – although the memories remain etched in his mind.

The banner progressed around the country with public handover ceremonies and finished up in London for a parade in the grounds of Buckingham Palace before the Queen and Prince Philip on 22 July, with 1,500 cadets from ACF and CCF.

Above: The Duke of Edinburgh presents the ACF Banner on 8 July 2005 at Royal Military Academy Sandhurst

Above: Mike Gerrish in 1960 carrying the banner for 2nd Battalion Northumberland ACF during its presentation at the ACF's centenary

Frimley Park visit, 2008

HRH The Duke of Edinburgh's last official engagement with the ACF was a visit to the Cadet Training Centre Frimley Park, on 17 October 2008, to mark the 50th anniversary of its foundation.

His Royal Highness conveyed thanks and praise to all those involved who helped make the visit so enjoyable. He was particularly impressed by the standard of the parade which was achieved only as part of a five-day course that participants had been attending at Frimley Park. He also appreciated his subsequent tour of the Training Centre.

Photos of HRH The Duke of Edinburgh at the 50th anniversary of Frimley Park, taken by Sergeant Dan Harmer, Captain Michael Nolan and Major Oliver Shepard

A final tribute, 2021

HRH The Duke of Edinburgh was laid to rest during a Ceremonial Royal Funeral at St George's Chapel in the grounds of Windsor Castle. Pipe Major Colour Sergeant and former cadet Peter Grant had the privilege of playing a moving lament at the ceremony.

It was the last, and most emotional, time the former cadet played for HRH The Duke of Edinburgh, and any stress he felt leading up to the moment was dissipated by the presence of HM The Queen and a grieving Royal Family.

'There was a lot of pressure prior to playing and I was well aware that the cameras were about to broadcast my performance to millions around the world,' he said.

'After spending time in St George's Chapel before playing, I felt a sense of emotion and sadness for HM The Queen and the Royal Family. My sole focus was to play well for everybody at the service – the cameras became an afterthought.'

Peter, of 4th Battalion The Royal Regiment of Scotland (4 SCOTS), was all too aware when he took up his post a year ago that this honour might fall to him: the current 4 SCOTS Pipe Major at the time of the Duke of Edinburgh's

Former cadet, Pipe Major Colour Sergeant Peter Grant had the privilege of playing a moving lament at the Duke of Edinburgh's funeral

© Crown Copyright

death is destined to take the role of piper at his funeral service. The beautiful and touching piece of music was *The Flowers of the Forest*, a funeral tune of The Royal Regiment of Scotland.

'It is an incredibly emotional tune for many people,' he said.

Peter met the Duke of Edinburgh on several occasions, particularly because Prince Philip was the Royal Colonel of 4 SCOTS.

'He presented the Battalion with our new Regimental Colours and presented us with our Operation Herrick medals after a tour of Afghanistan.

'Every time we met him, he was very engaging, forthcoming and would mingle with the troops. I loved his sense of humour; he

always put you at ease which made every encounter memorable.

'I have early memories of seeing Prince Philip when, as a young boy, I played at the Braemar Gathering – the village I come from. That's one of the reasons I felt so emotional [at the funeral]; he's been part of my life for as long as I can remember.'

Peter was a cadet in 2 Highlanders ACF where he was part of the Pipes and Drums before starting his military career.

He says: *'I'd recommend a career as a piper or drummer in the Army to any cadet. It's a highly rewarding career with unique opportunities. You can travel the world and create memories which will stay with you forever. If I could begin my career and do it all over again, I would.'*

Due to the pandemic, some elements of the Duke of Edinburgh's funeral in the grounds of Windsor Castle on 17 April were modified and scaled back. However, the day was still very much in line with Prince Philip's wishes.

Colonel Clint Riley said: *'Everyone who watched HRH The Duke of Edinburgh's funeral was moved by the occasion; it had his detailed planning which the armed services carried out in great style.*

'Sadly, no members of the ACF were present, but we will say our own farewells to our Colonel-in-Chief of 68 years at a future date. Many of those who

were on parade were former cadets themselves: one who had a key appointment was former Cadet RSM Joshua Ward of Lincolnshire ACF who is now Corporal Joshua Ward REME. He was the standby driver of the specially converted Land Rover Defender.'

Another former cadet who played a part in the service was George Whyte of the Queen's company of the Grenadier Guards. George, who turned 23 on the date of the funeral, was chosen alongside seven fellow grenadiers to perform the role of coffin bearer. A former Sandy Secondary School student, he joined the Army Cadets aged 12, before going to Army Foundation College, Harrogate aged 16.

The Duke of Edinburgh's Award

An enduring legacy

Army cadets have been participating in the DofE Award since its inception in 1956 and, for more than 60 years, cadets and CFAVs had the privilege of meeting HRH The Duke of Edinburgh in person.

Photo: Paul Lincoln

Army Cadets and the Duke of Edinburgh's Award have been intertwined since the inception of the Award.

A large number of cadets undertake the Award as part of their training and have also played an important role in the DofE's most prestigious events, including its 50th Anniversary in 2006 and Diamond Anniversary in 2016.

Liz Green, SO2 DofE, HQ Army Cadets says: *'Our cadets have taken part in expeditions across the globe, volunteered in their local communities, and developed new skills and their own physical fitness through undertaking the Award.*

'Currently, around 6,000 cadets and adult volunteers take part in the programme every year, with around 2,000 gaining Bronze, Silver and Gold DofE Awards.

'Each year, around 100 cadets and CFAVs travel to one of the Royal Palaces to be presented with their Gold Award. Although these have been presented by the Earl of Wessex or another member of the Royal Family since 2017, many of our cadets and CFAVs have fond memories of meeting Prince Philip at their Award presentation in earlier times.

'As we reflect on the legacy that HRH The Duke of Edinburgh has left us, we are more determined than ever to ensure every cadet is given the opportunity to take part in and complete their Award in the Army Cadets.'

» The Duke of Edinburgh's 'favourite cadet'

In 2016, ex-cadet Emmalee Wray remembers feeling extremely excited to meet HM The Queen and HRH The Duke of Edinburgh after she was selected as the Queen's Cadet.

Emmalee, formerly a cadet with Ballymena Detachment of the ACF, says: *'After achieving my Bronze and Silver DofE Awards within the Cadets, I couldn't wait to be working towards my Gold. I chose netball as my sport and singing as my skill.'*

After completing residential training at Ballykinler in County Down, she discovered she had been selected to represent the ACF at the Queen's 90th birthday beacon-lighting at Windsor Castle.

'I found out I would be walking by the Queen's side to represent Northern Ireland at the official birthday party in Windsor Castle,' she says.

The Queen's 90th birthday was marked on 21 April 2016 with a nationwide chain of beacons and Her Majesty lit the first beacon at Windsor Great Park.

'On the Queen's first attempt the beacon didn't light, and the Duke of Edinburgh turned to us and whispered: "Has anybody got a match?". Another instance of his wit was when he asked me and an RAF Air Cadet if we had done the DofE Award scheme. I replied that I had and it was one of the reasons I was there. The other cadet truthfully revealed he hadn't and The Duke of Edinburgh responded by saying I was now his favourite cadet.'

As a cadet, Emmalee gained qualifications and had many great experiences, including a six-week Canadian exchange. She was presented her Gold DofE Award at St James's Palace, London.

The former Ballymena Academy pupil was accepted at Newcastle University where she joined the University Officer Training Corps. She is now finishing her Postgraduate Certificate in Education, has recently passed her Army Officer Selection Board and will attend Royal Military Academy Sandhurst in September.

'Meeting HM The Queen and HRH The Duke of Edinburgh was something I'll never forget – it never would have happened if it were not for the Army Cadets.'

» Royally tongue-tied

AUO Ros Whyall, County DofE Officer for Cambs ACF was awarded a Gold Duke of Edinburgh's Award on 7 November 2003. She says:

'I completed my expedition in Germany due to the foot and mouth outbreak in the UK at the time. During my presentation the Duke of Edinburgh was particularly interested in those who had completed their expeditions abroad. I raised my hand and he asked where my expedition had been and, much to my embarrassment, I couldn't remember. Fortunately someone in my presentation group was able to come to my rescue – it was in Wolfsburg, near Hanover.

'The DofE Award had a hugely positive impact on my life and I was able to complete all three levels. It provided me with independence, confidence, problem-solving skills and lifelong friends. It introduced me to new hobbies, sports, interests and helped me secure my first job.

'Now, as a County DofE Officer, I'm privileged to be able to support others in their Award and watch them gain new skills and accomplishments.'

Ros Whyall as a cadet (above) and today.

Army Cadets in
October 2020

» New Chief of Staff

Colonel John Boyd OBE was announced as Army Cadets' new Chief of Staff, following Brigadier Stuart Williams' appointment as Deputy Commander Cadets.

Colonel John spent over 30 years in the Army, with most of his regimental duty in the Parachute Regiment. More recently he worked at Army HQ in Andover. He said:

'It's a real thrill to be joining the Army Cadets at such an unprecedented time in its history. I'm very much looking forward to working with young people and delivering opportunities that will set them up for life. I am passionate about training and keen to deliver an exciting syllabus.'

» Female soldiers online

WO2 Jody Mardling of MI Battalion (pictured) spoke to cadets from Merseyside ACF about her career in the British Army during a virtual instalment of the *Cadet Talks With Female Soldiers* series.

Jody revealed memories of training prior to joining the Army, told stories about her sporting experiences and time spent in Germany, Canada and Cyprus, and shared what it was like to be deployed to Iraq and Afghanistan.

The talk was followed by a Q&A session, which gave cadets the opportunity to find out more, including what it was like being one of the only females on deployment.

She highlighted the positive changes the organisation has made since she joined: *'It's more inclusive now and a lot of the courses you do can transfer to civilian qualifications. There's a variety of different courses available – mental health, first aid, mindfulness, coaching and mentoring. It's bigger and better.'*

'We pitched a tent in the living room to add atmosphere'

Photo: Daniel Turner

» Rising to the challenge

Army Cadets Assistant PR Officer Lucy Davis ascended the highest peak in South Wales during the pandemic. It was a remarkable achievement given that, nine years ago, Lucy was told she might be in a wheelchair for the rest of her life.

Due to her long-term health problems, Lucy was advised to shield during the early days of the pandemic, but boredom soon set in and, while posting ACF social media, she found herself inspired by cadets' activities.

She started her adventure at home, completing the Pen y Fan stair challenge in which she climbed the height of the mountain on her staircase. *'We pitched a tent in the living room to add atmosphere,'* she said.

Then, when shielding rules changed, she accompanied her husband on the running challenge. Finally, inspired by Army Cadets National Ambassador Sally Orange's Pen y Fan climb, Lucy took on the ultimate challenge and climbed to the top of the mountain in real life.

Award for cadet

Corporal Conway from Lothian and Borders ACF received the West Lothian Armed Forces Day Somme Company (Coy) Cadet Of The Year Award.

Somme Coy Commander, Captain Colin Jamieson, said to Corporal Conway: *'We are very proud of you. Every night you turn up in smart uniform and put your heart and soul into every activity.*

'You're a fine example of "you get out of the Army Cadet Force what you put in". To the rest of the cadets: this could be you next year – keep working hard!'

ADVENTURERS

Bear Grylls shares the ethos that's helped him achieve some incredible feats during his career, while Tracy Edwards MBE reveals what she learnt taking part in the world's toughest ocean race. Think you could climb El Cap at 13? Ella Kirkpatrick did; she reveals what went down.

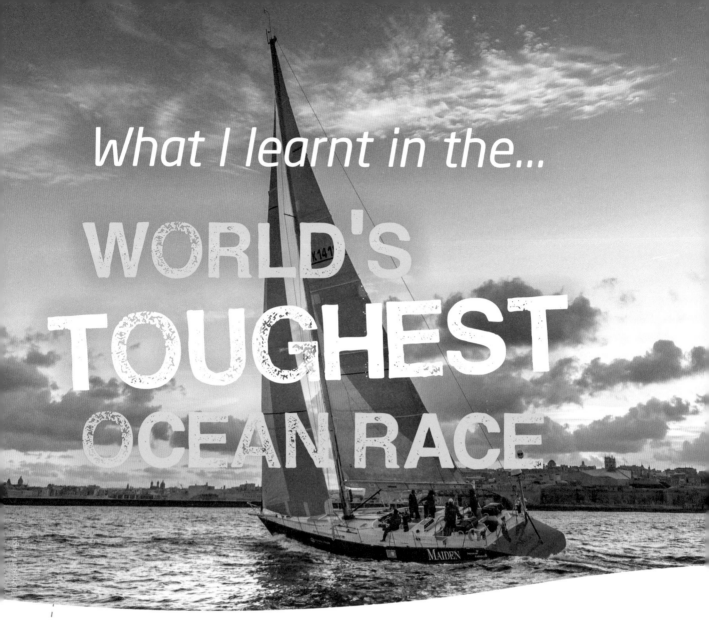

What I learnt in the...
WORLD'S TOUGHEST OCEAN RACE

Tracy Edwards MBE captured the world's attention when, in 1989, she and her all-female crew defied critics by winning two legs (and coming second overall in their class) in the Whitbread Round The World Race. It was the best result for a British crew since 1977 and is still unbeaten. What did she learn from the experience?

Find your niche

At the age of 16, after being bullied at school and finding things difficult at home, Tracy dropped out of formal education and ended up working as a stewardess on a yacht in Greece.

'In the 17 years leading up to getting on my first boat, I had never felt too comfortable about who I was or how I fitted in to this universe. Yet when I first went to sea, I felt I had found my tribe and my natural habitat – it was what I had been looking for.'

Criticism can spur you on

Tracy faced derision and prejudice when she announced her dream to skipper the first all-female crew in the world's toughest ocean challenge. Very few people believed an all-female crew would be able to complete the 33,000 mile race, and no-one was willing to risk sponsoring them.

'Hallelujah for the critics because all they did was make us more determined', says Tracy, *'though at the time it was quite disheartening. I remember a headline saying: "Back to the kitchen sink, girls – you've failed".'*

'The crew survived icebergs, -30 degree temperatures, frostbite, satellite signal failure and no food for days'

Left: Maiden in the Mediterranean. Above: Tracy Edwards

Photo: The Maiden Factor

Believe in yourself

Tracy remortgaged her house to buy a *'wreck of a boat with a pedigree'*. Then, over six months, she and her team used borrowed tools to rip Maiden apart and rebuild her.

'I was riddled with doubt but gradually learnt to have confidence in myself. I used to think if something felt easy then I must have missed something.

'I'd already trained professionally and raced in the Whitbread Round the World Race as a crew member so, for 12 years, I had absorbed a lot of information. I began to realise I did actually know this stuff.'

Leadership can be learned

Thanks to the vision of HM King Hussein of Jordan a sponsor was found for Maiden, but there was still a question over who should skipper her.

'When I realised I was going to have to skipper her as well as everything else, the panic set in,'

says Tracy. *'I thought, I've got to learn how to be a leader – surely that's something you're born with? But I discovered leadership can be learnt.*

'I learnt how to be a project manager, a fundraiser and a PR person – luckily, I was surrounded by people willing to teach me.'

We're capable of more than we think

On 2 September 1989, Maiden squared up on the starting line of the Whitbread Race and set off amid a 22-strong fleet of boats. During the race, the crew survived icebergs, -30 degree temperatures, frostbite, satellite signal failure and no food for several days.

'It was cold, wet and miserable but that's just a process you go through,' says Tracy. *'When you are focused on your mission, goal and passion, and you have that need to beat the other teams, you almost don't notice the discomfort.*

'I remember a headline saying: "Back to the kitchen sink, girls - you've failed"'

Photo: Michael Chester

Above: Tracy (centre) and the original crew celebrate after their win. Left: original crew reunion at St Katherine's Docks

'You train for it, practise, process, plan and prepare so, by the time you leave, you're ready. You know you've taken care of everything within your control, which gives you the ability to deal with the unexpected.'

It takes time to process big life-events

The Maiden returned to Southampton to a rapturous welcome from thousands of supporters. The crew had confounded critics and amazed doubters: not only did they win two of the hardest legs, they also came second overall in their class.

'We weren't quite prepared for the level of adulation, success, fame and everything else which came within the space of a few hours,' admits Tracy. 'I didn't deal with that very well. We were one of the first teams to become famous and there wasn't a lot of celebrity around sport at the time.

'I had a breakdown after the race and learnt the hard way that we needed to give ourselves time to process what had been an extraordinary experience. I didn't allow myself to do that, which was a huge lesson.'

Use your passion to serve others

In 2014, Tracy learnt that Maiden was rotting in the Seychelles, so she set about raising funds to bring her back to the UK. With support from HRH Princess Haya Bint Al Hussein, Maiden was shipped to Southampton and an extensive refit began.

'Maiden changed my life and I wanted to change the lives of other girls'

Tracy then set up charity The Maiden Factor Foundation and, in 2018, embarked on a three-year world tour with a new all-female crew to raise awareness and funds for girls' education.

'Maiden changed my life and I wanted to change the lives of other girls,' she says. *'Today, when we sail Maiden into port, young women look at the physical proof of what a girl can do when just one person believes in her. Maiden is inspiring and has this extraordinary effect on people: they come down to the boat and feel a sense of what is possible.'*

Education is life changing

Tracy continues to work with communities around the world to ensure girls have access to education.

'The education of girls is essential to every problem we have and, when you really drill down and look at the figures from the UN, UNESCO and UNICEF, if every girl in the world had 12 years of education we would have the very real possibility of ending world poverty and stopping the spread of viruses.

'When you educate a girl you increase the socio-economic status of her family, community, village and country. It's also been proved that in areas where girls are educated, people are happier – which is wonderful.'

Keep moving forward

Tracy could never have predicted where that particular voyage would take her, but it taught her the importance of taking action. She says, *'There are two certainties in life: if you stand still nothing will happen but if you keep moving forward something* will *happen.*

'It doesn't even matter if you go in the wrong direction, or don't know where you are going; if you are on the move you are more likely to find out where you are supposed to be, rather than sitting around waiting for it.'

Go further

1. Find out more about Tracy's work at themaidenfactor.org.

2. Watch the movie (scan the QR code) Maiden's story has been captured in an inspiring documentary film, *Maiden.* It reveals incredible original at-sea footage of Tracy and her team, and tells the tale of the barriers they smashed and the success they achieved against all odds.

What I learnt ...
CLIMBING EL CAP
AGED 13

Ella Kirkpatrick was a regular kid from Sheffield with little climbing experience when she became one of the youngest females to climb El Capitan, the iconic 1,000-metre wall in Yosemite National Park, USA.

Ella was accompanied by a team of five experienced climbers, including her dad – pro climber and mountaineer Andy Kirkpatrick – and ex Royal Marine sniper Aldo Kane. The six-day adventure was recorded by the BBC.

Watch the film of Ella's adventure here »

» How did you come to undertake such an astonishing feat?

At the time we did it, my dad had climbed El Cap 22 times (he's now climbed it about 30 times, including doing it solo) and it was his signature mountain to climb. It's a massive landmark; when you see it, you always know what it is.

We'd go to his talks and slide shows about his climbing adventures and, as we were leaving one of the shows, a fan came up and said: *'When are you going to climb El Cap then, Ella?'* and Dad said jokingly:

'Oh, she'll have to wait until she's 13.' But later in conversation, I asked him, *'Could I actually climb El Cap?'* and he said, *'You know, maybe that would be a good idea.'*

Sometime after that, a filmmaker my dad knew suggested we do it as a TV programme with the idea of me climbing El Cap with Aldo Kane – the story being about the contrast between a 13-year-old girl and a former Royal Marine who were both climbing it for the first time. That fell through, as media things often do, but I pulled the "mum card" with Dad, saying, *'It's alright Dad, Mum said it wouldn't have happened anyway because you're unreliable',* and he said, *'Right, we're going!'*

We decided to do it by ourselves, but then it got picked up by CBBC. Then Aldo decided to come along too, so it was me, Aldo, my dad, Ben Pritchard (who filmed it) and my dad's best mate Paul Tattersall. My mum said I could only go if Paul went too, as she knew nothing would happen to me if both my dad and Paul were there.

» Did you have any worries about agreeing to do it?

No, I just thought it would be fun and I was just thrilled to get a holiday out of it. I got three weeks off school, so I didn't even care that it was going to be turned into a TV show. As a 13 year old I was just so excited to go to America and that my brother wouldn't be there!

> **'El Cap isn't vertical – it's an overhang, so a lot of the time I was away from the wall'**

» What happened when you arrived in Yosemite?

We were there for about a week before we went up: we were scouting it out, shopping and regrouping. I asked Dad if we should go climbing to practise and he said, *'No, we'll be fine,'* so in terms of what I did in preparation, it was nothing beyond trying out the gear.

We were on the mountain for six days in total. We slept at the bottom, climbed up [the group took the Tangerine Trip route], slept on portaledges [a hanging tent system designed for rock climbers who spend multiple days and nights on a big wall] for four nights, then camped at the top overnight before making our way down again.

» How much previous climbing experience did you have?

Little to none. Mum and Dad are divorced and whenever we went to visit Dad in Scotland (where he lived when we were younger), we didn't go climbing because his girlfriend at the time [Karen Darke, MBE, British Paralympic gold medalist and adventurer] was in a wheelchair so it wasn't something we did as a family. I'd lead-climbed a route on a climbing wall, which is reasonably hard, but I'd really had very little experience at all.

» It's a notoriously difficult wall to climb ...

Yes it is, but El Cap isn't vertical – it's an overhang, so a lot of the time I was away from the wall. To climb it you'd have to be one of those big climbers like Tommy Caldwell [Tommy made the first free ascents of several El Capitan routes]. My dad doesn't even climb it. He does what's called aiding – he puts the gear in and pulls himself up. So I let them put the gear in and I climbed up the ropes, doing thousands of pull-ups to get to the top.

One thing we hadn't counted on was how tired I'd be. I did minimal exercise at home (apart from a few clubs I went to) and was so physically exhausted between the pitches I'd stop on the portaledge and have a little nap. There wasn't really any hand-and-feet climbing except for the last pitch, which I wanted to do because I was sick of pulling myself up. My dad said afterwards, '*You know that's the most dangerous pitch for you to have climbed?*' and I just said, '*Oh, that's interesting.*'

» How did you cope with the fear when swinging hundreds of feet up in the air?

It was fine. In the TV show they made a drama out of an incident where the rope got tangled under the portaledge, but in reality it was okay because of the trust I had in my dad. My biggest fear was having to wee and poo on a mountain.

» How does that work?

You're still attached on your waist but you pull your leg straps down and just have a wee into the abyss. And I did wee on my dad – and the cameraman ... it was bound to happen. As the only girl I thought the others had it easy.

The three men would camp in one spot, then me and Dad would camp on the pitch below (it's not too safe to have all five on one anchor). But the one night I needed to have a poo turned out to be when all five of us camped together. It was pretty awful. Dad blasted some music and I just had to do it into a bag. That was my lowest moment.

» How did the team work together?

We were split into two camps. Paul and Aldo led, while my dad did a lot of the heavy lifting – he hauled up the bags and set us up. Ben and I were like buddies, moving up the mountain at the same time. We all had walkie talkies to communicate with each other.

I don't think Aldo had climbed a big wall like El Cap before, although he used to work on wind turbines so he was used to heights. He was out of his comfort zone though; the whole time he seemed petrified. He enjoyed it afterwards, I'm sure, but I don't think he did at the time.

I wish they'd made the me vs Aldo programme as that would have been so interesting. I was so chilled, taking it in my stride as they lowered me out into the nothingness, floating 20 metres away from the wall.

It was more difficult for Aldo because he had a harder job than me but also, because of my age, I had total trust in everyone. I'd known them all – except Aldo – from birth, so I had a kind of blind ignorance, thinking, *It'll be fine.*

» You had to carry provisions for six days. What did you take?

Bagels, bagels and more bagels – and cream cheese. We were allowed to have a can of pop each day as it's rehydrating and that was our treat. The night before we got to Yosemite we stayed in this seedy motel and had a burrito which was so huge I had to throw half of it away. Then the entire time I was on the mountain all I could think about was that burrito – I was fixated on it.

» What was it like sleeping on a portaledge?

I was so exhausted from doing so many pull-ups each day that it was easy to sleep. You stay in your harness so you're safe, but you are at least allowed to take your helmet off which is a great relief.

» How did it feel to get to the top?

I can relate the sense of accomplishment to other things I've achieved in my life, like getting my GCSEs, my A levels and my degree [last year Ella was awarded a first class honours degree in maths].

It was an amazing feeling, like finishing your last exam … except you have to get down, which is just as dangerous as getting up. You walk and abseil down the back of the mountain and it takes a whole day. We left early in the morning and it was dark when we got down. Then we went for a massive pizza.

» Did it help you understand your dad's obsession with climbing that big wall?

I totally got it, which was good for our relationship. I'd often wondered why he did it but, seeing it firsthand, I understood. People are drawn to El Cap; it's an icon.

» What did you learn from the trip?

When I went home to Sheffield afterwards I thought, *Why am I here? There's so much more out there. The world is a massive place and I can have an amazing life if I want.* It really opened my eyes.

I felt a real sadness when I was home. It was such an intense experience and I met some amazing people in Camp Four, which is the camp the climbers stay in. We've been back since and it's the coolest place – and because I'd climbed the mountain I was one of the cool kids.

It helped me learn to manage my expectations, especially after getting let down the first time with the TV programme. Then, when I got there, El Cap was bigger than I thought it was going to be, the experience harder than I expected, and the reward (because we'd achieved it together) bigger than I could have imagined.

Go further

Female and interested in doing more physical activity?

Army Cadets are proud supporters of the This Girl Can campaign. Read more here »

BEAR GRYLLS

In August, ahead of his Gone Wild Festival, we tracked down the TV adventurer and got his tips on how to tackle life's challenges.

If you've seen the TV series *Running Wild with Bear Grylls*, you'll know he takes famous personalities (Zac Efron, Channing Tatum, Kate Winslet and President Obama to name a few) out into the wild for adventures. Many of the celebs featured in the programmes feel daunted by the unknown.

'We have so many people who arrive unsure and a bit nervous,' he says. 'That's part of all of our journeys in life and in the wild. You've got to face those scarier moments and keep

'The good stuff lies on the other side of fear'

moving towards them. When we do, we get strength and pride which can last a lifetime.'

Everyone, he feels, has the potential to embrace scary situations.

'Fear is always going to be part of our lives but it's there to keep us on our toes and help us perform.

'I've learnt the way to manage it and turn it into positive energy is to keep doing scary stuff every day. By doing that we get familiar with fear and begin to be able to control it. And our ability to use that fear becomes stronger with repetition.

'Life will always throw up obstacles and it's key to learn how to embrace those situations. That's why adventure is so powerful – you're constantly faced with new and scary problems to master.'

To Inspire To Achieve

>> Make friends with failure

Bear doesn't just encourage embracing fear, he also recommends making friends with failure.

'Having to deal with multiple failures is part of life; I always feel the only real failure is in giving up.

'When we fail we should treat it as a rite of passage, a key marker on our way to success. After all, the good stuff lies on the other side of fear, pain, struggle and failure. Nothing that's worth doing is easy, but when you get there it's so sweet.'

>> Avoid dream stealers

He warns young people to avoid individuals he calls 'dream stealers'.

'Dream stealers are people who tell you that you can't do something. NEVER listen to them! But use that negativity to fire you onwards. The world is full of underdogs who've achieved incredible things, and they will all have been told a thousand times their dream was unachievable. Champions determine their own destiny and never give up.'

Bear, who has three sons, shares his hopes for them.

'I just want them to be kind, throw themselves at life and be resilient in the storms they'll face,' he says. *'Life isn't about awards and achievements. It's about the friends you have and the memories you make.'*

>> Remember the positives

The pandemic has been incredibly difficult for many, but he urges young people to remember the positives too.

'There have been many good things amid the pain, so it's good to remember those as the storm passes. Families have spent more time together, we've become more active, and many are now seeking out adventures here in the UK. We've also learnt to be grateful for simple things and to re-evaluate life's real heroes.'

Photo: Fabian Equey

The Bear necessities

Bear Grylls OBE is one of the most recognisable faces of survival and outdoor adventure. He trained from a young age in martial arts and spent three years as a soldier in the British Special Forces as part of 21 SAS Regiment. It was there he mastered many of the survival skills for which he's become famous. His achievements include:

- Being one of the youngest climbers to reach the summit of Mount Everest.

- Starring in seven seasons of Discovery Channel's *Man vs. Wild* – one of the most-watched shows on the planet.

- Hosting more extreme adventure TV shows than anyone. They include *Running Wild with Bear Grylls*, interactive Netflix show *You vs Wild* and National Geographic series *Hostile Planet*.

- Winning two BAFTAs for his Channel 4 show *The Island with Bear Grylls*.

- Spending 15 weeks at Number 1 in the *Sunday Times* bestseller list for his autobiography *Mud, Sweat and Tears*. He's written 95 books.

- Being an Honorary Colonel to the Royal Marines Commandos, and the first Chief Ambassador of World Scouting.

- Eating everything from insects and raw snake to the heart of a moose and goat testicles in the wild.

- His motto is 'courage and kindness … and never give up!'

Acquire skills for life

As Chief Scout in the UK, Bear thinks the organisations and activities young people take part in outside the classroom are as important as academic success, which is why he's helped launch an education initiative for schools, called BecomingX.

'I struggled at school but, as I got older, I discovered a love of the military and adventure, and that was where I flourished. The school curriculum so often fails to empower and teach relevant skills.'

» A new adventure

August 2021 saw the launch of a festival, created by Bear, to appeal to those with a thirst for excitement as insatiable as his own. The Gone Wild Festival, which took place at Powderham Castle in Devon, was packed with adrenalin-filled activities such as coasteering, wakeboarding, abseiling and climbing, as well as featuring live music from Kaiser Chiefs, Melanie C and Razorlight.

Developed in coordination with former Commandos and in support of The Royal Marines Charity, the event provided a fun weekend for families seeking out new adventures.

Young people and adults had the chance to learn essential survival skills such as shelter building, fire lighting and campfire cooking with expert instructors from the Bear Grylls Survival Academy.

» World-famous explorers

The inclusion of world-famous explorers and adventurers in the festival line up was a big draw and headline names included TV explorer Steve Backshall, boxer Nicola Adams, *Blue Peter* presenter Ayo Akinwolere and Army Cadet Champion 'Big Phil' Campion (right, on stage).

'Phil is both a hero and a friend,' says Bear. *'He does such great work within the Army Cadets and I know how much he loves inspiring young people.'*

> **» For information about the next Gone Wild Festival visit gonewildfestival.com**

GONE WILD

Highlights from the festival

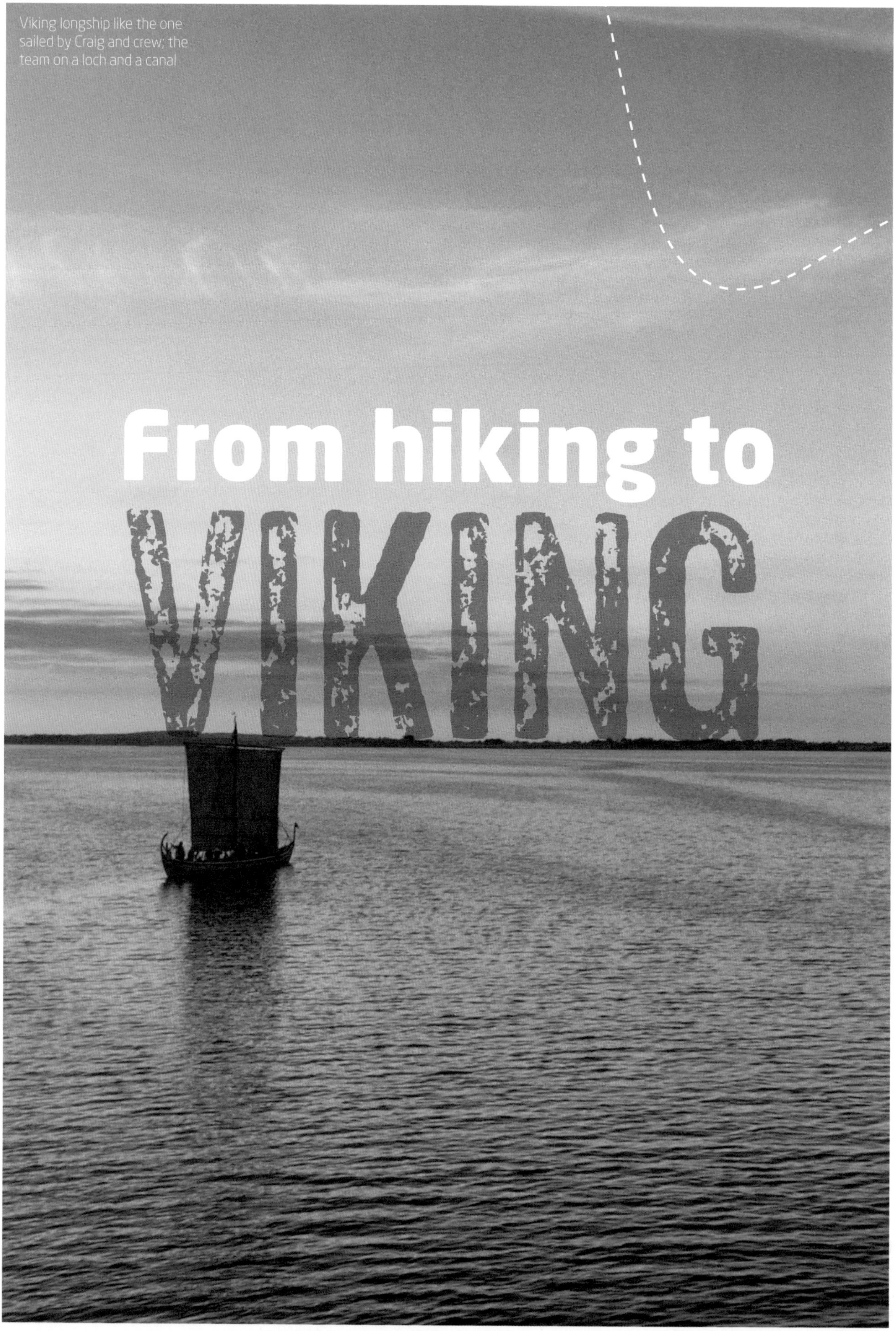

From hiking to VIKING

To Inspire To Achieve

Each year, polar explorer and Army Cadets National Ambassador **Craig Mathieson** takes a group of young people on a gruelling and life-changing trek through the Arctic. But what do you do when planes and travel plans are grounded in a pandemic? You take a Viking longship through the middle of Scotland, of course ...

Photo: A360DEGREES

Never one to be deterred from achieving his objective, Craig Mathieson wasn't going to let a global pandemic stop him from taking his latest Polar Academy intake on a life-altering adventure.

Of course, trekking across the Arctic was somewhat off the cards during the height of the pandemic, so Craig thought outside the box *'and I managed to get my hands on a Viking longship which we took through Scotland'*, he says.

'It was actually the first time a Viking longship has been through *Scotland and it was probably the only expedition to take place in the UK in the first half of 2021.'*

The adventure started on the west coast of Scotland and the team rowed through the canal system and lochs out to the east coast. It was five days of brutally tough rowing and sailing for Craig, the Polar Academy guides and a 14-strong group of 15-to-17-year-old Scottish teenagers.

Even when it was over, they had to walk over the mountains for three days before finally catching a lift home in a helicopter.

As with the annual Arctic expeditions, the aim was to take a group of young people who've experienced tough times and train them to undertake an incredibly challenging feat (both physically and mentally) to prove to themselves just what they're capable of. This group who took part in the Viking longship expedition was from Bell Baxter High School in Cupar, Fife.

'As they missed the Arctic trip (twice – the first time the trip was cancelled just ten days before we were due to set off) this was the best thing we could come up with that could take place in this country', says Craig.

'Just to get to see a Viking longship is a thrill, and it's quite a famous one; you'll have seen it in films – it's just been used in Outlaw King *in which Robert Pine plays Robert The Bruce.'*

The logistics of doing this alternative mission were possibly as challenging as getting a group to the Arctic.

'The boat was in Glasgow so we had to use a huge crane to get it out of the water, then put it on a massive lorry and drive it to the west coast', says Craig. Then, at the end, they had to do the same to get it back to Glasgow.

Of course, Covid provided plenty of additional challenges: the group were in a strict bubble and, when wild camping, had to sleep in separate tents to be Covid-compliant. Even when they stayed overnight on commercial campsites Craig had to hire the entire site to ensure no one else could enter and inadvertently scupper the mission by passing on the virus.

'We don't say this is what we want to do, we say this is what we're going to do. And once they've got that attitude they're unstoppable'

Nothing was left to chance, including the young people's ability to actually get through such a gruelling experience. In preparation for the event, Craig and his guides put the youngsters through incredible cardio, circuit and endurance training. This included hauling tyres through water and over sand *'until they were almost at elite-athlete standard of fitness, when at the start they'd had no fitness at all'.*

Having the confidence to take on the expedition and see it through was just as important.

'You have to remember a lot of these kids have been through a really major trauma or come from very difficult backgrounds, so their confidence is shattered. We are starting with little shells of people, and we build them up really slowly.

'The key is to give them huge objectives, which they can't even comprehend initially, like taking an expedition to the Arctic where no one has been

before, or rowing a longship through the middle of Scotland which no one has done before.

'We don't say this is what we want to do, we say this is what we're going to do. And once they've got that attitude they're unstoppable. We couldn't do the longship trip with adults; I think they'd give up.

'The boat actually has a regular crew and I was told by the skipper [who accompanied them on the expedition] *that they usually stop every 20 minutes because it's hard work rowing this three-and-a-half-tonne boat with its heavy oars. But that was too soon for our kids – they swapped every hour and a half. Some of the kids didn't want to swap out so they'd row for six or seven hours and be absolutely fine.*

'The thing with this sort of boat is that it doesn't move forward unless there is absolute teamwork with everyone using the same rowing style. It's extremely difficult.'

Beyond the adventures on the water is the importance of ensuring the experience has a long-lasting positive effect on the youngsters' lives.

'That's why we work with their families too. There's no point in changing the lives of these kids and then putting them back into a household that doesn't know what they've just been through.

'We call it the Legacy Team and every set of parents who have been through Polar Academy help the next set coming in, so it's like a family that grows year on year. What the kid achieves rubs off on the rest of the family.

Craig presenting awards to teenagers who took part in the expedition

What makes this project so unusual is the way the benefits keep rippling out through the community, way beyond the teenagers' families.

'Once they've finished their training, the teenagers go off into schools to share their experiences with others who are struggling, and tell them about where they were previously in their lives and where they are now. And that has a HUGE impact on kids.

'Meeting other teenagers they don't know – and our kids are usually properly "invisible" – and hearing about what they've done, well, they just sit there with their mouths open. Then they think, 'If she could do that, maybe I could do that'. That's the real power of it.

'They're not concentrating on the trauma; they're concentrating on moving forward'

'I always know when the Polar Academy kids have given a talk. I don't help them with it as it's their own story, but I find my inbox crammed with emails from parents saying their kid came home from school, where this young person spoke about The Polar Academy and what their doing in life now. They always say, "My child fits into that category: they're victims of bullying, or they've had some horrendous trauma in their life they can't get over."

'Doing an expedition like this doesn't make trauma disappear, but it puts these young people's lives back in focus where it needs to be. They're not concentrating on the trauma; they're concentrating on moving forward.'

» GO FURTHER

Simply scan the QR code to see the same Viking longship in the trailer for *Outlaw King*

Army Cadets in
November 2020

Photo: Daniel Turner Photography

» Remembrance Day went virtual

With many Remembrance Day parades and services cancelled due to the pandemic, cadets and CFAVs donned their uniforms and saluted from their doorsteps, sharing images online as part of the #doorstepsalute with The Remembrance Penny.

Lorraine Kelly, Army Cadets National Honorary Colonel, said: 'While Remembrance parades and events may look a bit different this year ... the #doorstepsalute

is a wonderful initiative for us all to participate in safely – at home on our doorsteps – as we honour the fallen who made the ultimate sacrifice.'

Cadets were also encouraged to upload videos, photographs, short stories or poems from family members who served the nation to The Remembrance Penny website.

To Inspire To Achieve

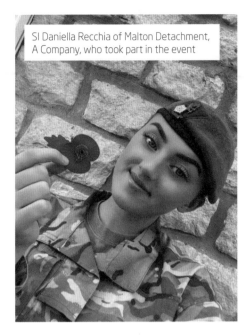
SI Daniella Recchia of Malton Detachment, A Company, who took part in the event

» Fantastic fundraising result

In the 14 days leading up to Remembrance Sunday, members of Yorkshire (North and West) ACF's A Company raised funds for the Royal British Legion. Between them they walked, cycled or ran, travelling the equivalent of the distance from John O'Groats to Land's End, the Cenotaph in London to the Somme Memorial in Thiepval and back to A Company HQ in Northallerton. They smashed the original target of 874 miles, amassing an incredible total distance of 1,895.6 miles.

The activities raised funds which will benefit the Royal British Legion by £760.

Project coordinator, Company Training Officer Captain Ben Porter said: *'Well done to all who took part. You have accomplished a tremendous task as a team, and done yourselves and your company proud. The amount raised for the Royal British Legion will help them with the financial, social, and emotional support they provide for millions of those who have served.'*

MAKE-UP OFF, GAME FACE ON.

#JoinTheAdventure
Armycadets.com

THIS GIRL CAN · ARMY CADETS GOING FURTHER

» This Girl Can

To boost the number of females participating in sports and typically male-dominated activities, Army Cadets teamed up with the This Girl Can campaign. Throughout the month we shared inspiring images and stories of female cadets who are also successful athletes.

» First aid in action

Lance Bombardier Shian Kennelly of Bedfordshire and Hertfordshire ACF, Hatfield Detachment, put her Army Cadets first-aid training into action when a classmate had a seizure. She put the pupil in the recovery position, asked fellow pupils to find teachers, called for an ambulance and monitored the situation.

Shian's sergeant, Max Fuller, said: *'Shian was brave and acted quickly to help the boy in need. We are amazingly proud of her as she did exactly what we taught her to do. We couldn't have asked more from her.'*

TAKE
THE TEST

Would you know what to do if you were caught in an avalanche or found yourself in the path of a tornado? And could your expedition and camping knowledge keep you out of danger? Time to find out ...

Take the test

Typical slab avalanche

Avalanche

The scenario

You and a friend have planned to mountaineer up one of Scotland's most stunning mountains in the Northern Cairngorms during winter.

It's the morning of the trip and there's been fresh snow in the night – although not much – and the sky is blue. You've got your packed lunch and kit laid out, and your friend is excitedly texting you to confirm the meeting time. You check the weather forecast and the Scottish Avalanche Information Service and read there's a risk of an avalanche today. What should you do?

Do you know how to avoid being caught up in an avalanche? Army Cadet National Ambassador and polar explorer **Craig Mathieson** gives his expert opinion.

A Call your friend and rearrange the trip for another day. It's not worth taking the risk.

B Decide to go for it but take crampons, ice picks, snow probes and transceivers with you to keep you safe.

C Talk it over with your friend and, if they're in agreement, go ahead – you don't get many days when you can get out into the mountains.

Avalanche
101

> 'There are many types of avalanche,' says Craig, 'from the loose-snow avalanche (where new snow tumbles down the mountain at 40mph) to those where airborne powder comes piling down at 175mph. The latter is the kind you see in the Alps.'

'We do get avalanches in the UK, especially in the Highlands of Scotland, the Welsh hills and the Lake District. These are usually slab avalanches where big slabs of snow break away and fall.

'In Scotland, we sometimes get wet avalanches in spring when the temperatures increase and the bonds between the snow and ground melt. Getting caught in that would be like being encased in concrete and the chances of survival slim.

'Despite what you might imagine, avalanches don't only happen on big mountains: a slope and snow is all that's required.'

Read more about different types of avalanche at beaware.sais.gov.uk.

Photo: A360DEGREES

> Polar explorer Craig has many years of military and mountaineering experience and has been involved in numerous expeditions to the Antarctic and Arctic. He runs The Polar Academy, a project that takes young people in Scotland on challenging and confidence-building expeditions to the Arctic.

Answer

'If there's a risk, don't go,' says Craig. 'Being caught in an avalanche is so dangerous you should always err on the side of caution.

'Preparation is everything in winter, so never just wake up and decide to head for the hills. Check the forecast. Even if the weather is stable and you decide to go, still take great care.

'That means never going out by yourself, and making sure those you go with have the same level of competence as you and know what to do in an emergency.

'Have the right kit: in winter you should take crampons, a shovel, avalanche probes, an ice axe and a transceiver so people can find you. Check the battery each time.

'It's especially important in winter to write details of the route you'll be taking and leave them with a responsible person. Agree a time by which you'll make contact when you're back and check they know to call 999 and ask for Mountain Rescue if you're late.

'When you get to the hill, check the local weather forecast for any weather changes – and have a plan B if you're not happy with the conditions.

'Everyone in your party should have a map and compass and know how to use them.

'Stay away from avalanche-prone areas – find a different route so you don't take any risks. If you see footprints in the snow that look like they've been made half an hour ahead, don't assume that's a safe route – they could have been lucky. Always do your own research.

'If you do get caught in an avalanche, shout or scream as loud as you can to alert others, while ditching your gear so you're not impaled on it. As you get caught up in the avalanche try to get to the side of it using a swimming motion or rolling, although that is incredibly difficult if you're being swept along at 40mph. Realistically, you have no control until the avalanche slows down.

'Close your mouth so you don't choke on snow and, as you come to a stop, make space around your head to help you breathe. Try to relax and conserve energy and oxygen. You probably won't know if you are upside down as it could be pitch black. You typically have 15 minutes (and up to an hour) to be found, but if you're the one searching never give up. People have managed to survive for 24 hours in Scotland.

'If you're a witness (not the one caught in the avalanche), track the person closely to identify the last place you see them before they disappear, taking a bearing against a tree or rock. Then get as many people to help search as quickly as possible.'

Visit the **Mountain Weather Information Service** to find weather info for mountain ranges across the UK. »

Take the test

Tornado

The scenario

You're on holiday visiting family friends who live in Oklahoma, USA. They take you for a drive in the countryside and you stop for a picnic. Seemingly out of nowhere, a fierce storm whips up around you and you notice something resembling a swirling funnel of air on the horizon.

Your American friends confirm it's a tornado. What should you do?

What would you do if faced with an oncoming tornado? Warning Coordination Meteorologist **Rick Smith** reveals the dos and don'ts.

A Get everyone to pile back in the car and ask the driver to put their foot down so the vehicle outruns the tornado. Take advantage of your head start by asking the driver to accelerate in the direction the tornado appears to be travelling.

B Guide your party to the nearest underpass or bridge and protect yourselves from the approaching tornado by creating a barricade with your possessions.

C Lead everyone to the nearest sturdy building and direct them to get as low to the ground as possible, and to cover their head and upper body.

The answer is C

» What is a tornado?

The Met Office describes a tornado (sometimes referred to as a twister) as a rapidly rotating column of air that reaches between the base of a storm cloud and the Earth's surface.

Tornadoes form in very unsettled weather as part of severe thunderstorms. Particular conditions need to be present for a tornado to occur and the result is a violently whirling mass of air, known as a vortex, which forms beneath the storm cloud.

A funnel cloud usually develops as the vortex forms due to the reduced pressure in the vortex. Strong inflowing winds intensify, and the spin rate increases as the vortex stretches vertically. If it continues stretching and intensifying for long enough the vortex touches the ground, at which point it becomes classified as a tornado. The tornado then moves across the surface causing severe damage or destruction to objects in its path.

Watch this Met Office video to find out more ...

» Where do tornadoes occur?

Around 30 tornadoes are reported in the UK each year and they can cause structural damage if they pass over built-up areas. Fortunately, tornadoes in the UK tend to be small, short-lived events that rarely threaten life.

In the States, however, it can be a very different matter. 'Tornado Alley', a region of Central USA, is particularly prone to violent tornado outbreaks which can be deadly.

In spring and summer, warm air from the Gulf of Mexico meets cool air from Canada in this region, leading to the formation of powerful storms known as supercells which, if the conditions are right, can spawn tornadoes.

See the kind of damage tornadoes can cause in this video ...

Answer

Warning Coordination Meteorologist Rick Smith from the NOAA National Weather Service Forecast Office in Norman, Oklahoma, stresses if you're outdoors and a tornado is approaching then it's best to seek shelter underground or inside a sturdy building.

'If one is available, try to get there,' he urges. *'Once you're in a building, you want to get as low as you can, staying away from outside walls, doors and windows. Cover your head and upper body with whatever you have – that's where you're most vulnerable to being injured by flying and falling debris.'*

If it's impossible to shelter in a building, Rick advises getting as low to the ground as possible.

'Find a ditch or ravine and lie flat, covering your head and upper body. Storms that cause tornadoes often come with very heavy rain, so be sure you're not taking cover in a flood-prone location.'

It may be human instinct to flee from danger, but it's not advisable to try and outrun a tornado in a car as high-speed tornado winds can blow large objects, including vehicles, hundreds of feet.

Hiding under a bridge or underpass may also seem a good idea, but meteorologists say that's one of the worst things you can do. Such structures can amplify the speed of winds and offer little to no protection from flying debris.

The best way to avoid having to make such life and death decisions in the moment, though, is to pay close attention to local weather forecasts before venturing out.

Rick adds: *'If severe thunderstorms are forecast, reconsider your plans to be outside. Stay close to a safe shelter in case a tornado warning is issued for the area of the USA you are visiting.'*

Take the test

How good is your expedition knowledge? Time to find out ...

1 What does the Countryside Code say about litter?

A It's fine to leave biodegradable items such as fruit peel but you should take plastic wrappers home with you.

B You should leave your rubbish in a neat pile where it can be picked up later by litter collectors.

C Leave no trace of your visit and take your litter home with you.

2 What's best practice when using a methylated spirit stove?

A Fill the stove from a small container instead of a bulk container and take the burner to the fuel, not the fuel to the burner.

B Be careful not to handle fuel near tents or naked flames; create a refuelling area away from the rest of the camp.

C Make sure, when refuelling a stove, the flame is completely extinguished and the stove cool.

Photo: Paul Bunce

3 What star-level expedition has a duration of two days and two nights with seven hours of activity per day?

A 2 star

B 3 star

C 4 star

To Inspire To Achieve

4 Foot care is essential on expedition. How can you look after your feet?

A Leave your boots on all the time, even at camp – if you take them off your feet can get puffy and you may not get the boots on again the next morning.

B Take your boots off when you get to camp and wear flip-flops or similar to give your feet an airing.

C Rub garlic cloves over your heels each night; its antibacterial properties can prevent blisters from becoming infected.

5 How should you store your sleeping bag at home?

A Rolled up in its stuffsack.

B Squashed into the bottom of your rucksack to stop it expanding and getting too bulky to carry on expedition.

C Hung up or in a bin bag: storing it in its stuffsack damages the filling.

6 An emergency occurs on an expedition which only has remote adult supervision. At what point should cadets call parents?

A Only once the incident is resolved and under the guidance of the supervisor. Ideally the supervisor would start the conversation with the parent and then hand over.

B After calling the supervisor, so parents can help.

C Parents should be the first call cadets make as emotions will be running high and parents can help calm things down.

7 The 'open access land' symbol denotes areas where you can wander at will without sticking to paths. What does it look like?

A

B

C

Take the test

Camping out with family and friends is a summer highlight, but being exposed to the elements isn't without potential risks. Take the test to see if you know how to avoid the most common hazards.

TENT

You're looking for the perfect spot to pitch your tent - which of these areas sounds ideal?

A A bank close to a moving stream: you'll have somewhere to clean the dishes and wash yourself.

B A sheltered spot, on level ground, where you can make certain the door is facing away from the wind.

C A stretch of grass in a valley at the bottom of a hill – which will provide excellent protection from the wind and sun.

Answer B. The most important consideration is to find a sheltered spot on flat ground – this can make the difference between a good night's rest and a camping nightmare.

Formal campsites provide level and safe plots on which to pitch your tent. Take advantage of natural windbreaks and position your tent so the door is facing away from the wind to avoid strong gusts.

If you're wild camping (make sure you have the landowner's permission) choose an area strewn with sand, grass or dirt rather than rocks and roots. Brush away any sticks, stones or tree branches which might poke you while you sleep.

Safety tip:
Never set up camp close to moving water and avoid low-lying areas as, if it rains, you risk waking up in a puddle – or worse, in a deadly flash flood.

FIRE

You plan to spend the evening toasting marshmallows around the campfire. Where should your family build the fire?

A An area next to trees where there is shelter from the elements, plus plenty of kindling and fuelwood.

B On a patch of dead grass – to avoid destroying growing vegetation.

C On a clearing of bare earth away from trees, bushes and plants, and at a safe distance from your tent.

Answer C. If you are on a campsite with a designated fire area, always use it. If your family is camping in a rugged area, your fire bed should be on bare earth not grass (especially dead grass) or near trees and vegetation. Dry grass, branches and bark catch fire extremely easily.

Safety tip: Keep flammables away from the fire and use rocks to build a non-flammable barrier around your fire.

STOVES

When using a portable stove to cook for your family, which of these safety measures should you follow?

A Choose a firm, level surface at ground level where the stove can't be knocked over. Make sure it's at least 3m away from flammable items and tents.

B Get everything you need together before starting to cook. Make it clear to your fellow campers when the stove is lit.

C Keep checking there is a flame, especially in bright sunlight, and never leave a lit stove unattended or unwatched.

Answer A, B and C. Even before your camping trip, make sure you're confident using your portable stove. Be aware of any dangers associated with the stove and know, in advance, what to do if it catches fire.

Safety tips: Never cook in a tent – fire can destroy a tent in under a minute. And never take a barbecue into a tent. Even a cooling barbecue gives off poisonous carbon monoxide which can kill.

TICKS

You've been for a walk in the woods and one of your party notices they have a tick (a tiny spider-like creature found in grass and woodlands) on their leg. What should you do?

A Remove the tick with petroleum jelly or butter.

B Use heat or ice to try and burn or freeze the tick.

C Use tweezers to remove the tick.

Answer C. Using tweezers, grasp the tick's head as close to the casualty's skin as you can. Gently pull the head upwards using steady even pressure. Do not jerk the tick as this may leave tick mouthparts embedded. Place the tick in a sealed plastic bag and give it to the casualty for identification. Encourage them to seek medical help if they feel unwell.

Safety tips: Cover your body when walking in woods and long grass, e.g. wear long-sleeved shirts and tuck your trousers into your socks. Keep to footpaths whenever possible, use insect repellent and wear light-coloured clothing (which'll help you spot a tick on them). On return, shower and check yourself for ticks.

To find out more about ticks scan the QR code.

NHS

» Cadets' Walking Home for Christmas success

Cadets got their walking boots on in December to help raise money for an important cause. Walking With The Wounded provides practical support for ex-service people: British military veterans who've served their country and been injured doing their job. It provides them with help and support to reintegrate into society, sustain their independence and find employment.

For a decade, Walking With The Wounded has provided this support, recognising the skills of armed service personnel and helping them transfer those skills into the civilian workplace. It has also assisted homeless veterans and those in the criminal justice system.

Money to pay for this important work is raised by organisations and individuals who take part in fundraising events such as the charity's Walking Home For Christmas campaign.

For the 2020 event, Army Cadets encouraged detachments to walk home from a significant distance between 10-20 December and, despite social distancing restrictions, the annual Christmas campaign was a triumph.

Army Cadets raised over £60,000 for the veterans' charity – the most money raised out of all the organisations taking part. Several detachments battled it out to score a top spot on the leaderboard.

Colonel Terry Hayter, National Sports and Development Manager ACF, said: 'It was great to watch the competitive spirit in action. Thank you all for supporting such a great cause.'

A special shout-out goes to Lance Corporal Niquita Potter of Devon ACF, Newton Abbot Detachment, who took part in the Walking Home For Christmas campaign. She said: 'I have Down's syndrome but I like to try and help others and achieve what I can, and I wanted to raise as much money by walking as far as I could.'

The 17-year-old walked 14 miles and raised over £1,300, smashing her initial target of £200.

» Leadership skills

CFAV Neil Jurd published an engaging and practical guide called *The Leadership Book*, a useful resource for anyone interested in leadership theory.

Neil gained significant leadership experience in his previous life as a British Army Officer leading troops in Iraq and as an instructor at Sandhurst. Since leaving the Army in 2009, he's worked in leadership development with clients including Commonwealth Games Team Scotland, the NHS and the Leadership Trust.

His guide is straightforward and easy to use and, rather than focusing heavily on academic theories, explores leadership themes in bite-size chunks. Ideas are brought to life through entertaining case studies and learning exercises.

The book offers a compassionate and values-driven approach to leadership, promoting inclusion, empathy and kindness. Neil presents leadership as a positive force which flows in all directions through high-performing organisations. He also makes a distinction between leadership and management and explains why it's important to have both.

NEWS IN BRIEF

❯ **Former cadet RSM Jack Goode**, (pictured above) of E Coy's Batley Detachment, took part in a passing out parade at the Royal Military Academy Sandhurst, having completed his officer training. He then became a commissioned officer in the Regular Army, less than 18 months after completing his time as a cadet with Yorkshire (North and West) ACF. Congratulations to Second Lieutenant Goode.

❯ **Cadet Colour Sergeant Morgan McCauley** of 28 Platoon, Broxburn, was named Most Inspirational Cadet in Scotland for 2020. CSgt McCauley has been a cadet for four years, during which time she has represented the battalion in cross country, athletics and swimming, as well as nationally representing the ACF in football and hockey.

❯ Undeterred by lockdown, members of **Derbyshire ACF** took their annual Christmas Concert online so it could be watched from living rooms across the UK. Videos of cadets performing individually were successfully pieced together to form a virtual band.

CHALLENGE

Want to learn how
to bodyboard? Think
you could master the art
of navigating by the stars?
Or perhaps you fancy
taking up bobsleigh?
Read on …

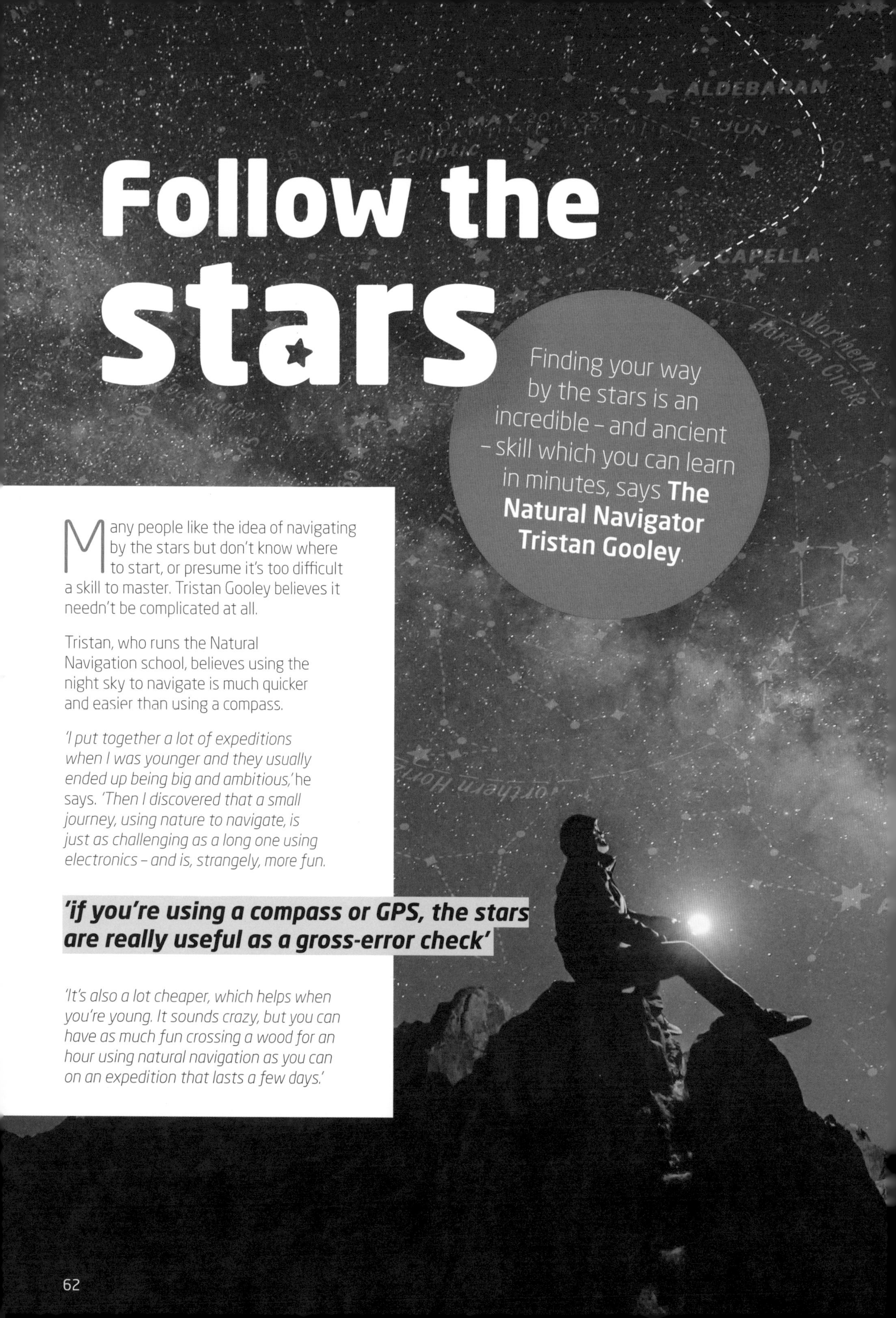

Follow the stars

Finding your way by the stars is an incredible – and ancient – skill which you can learn in minutes, says **The Natural Navigator Tristan Gooley**.

Many people like the idea of navigating by the stars but don't know where to start, or presume it's too difficult a skill to master. Tristan Gooley believes it needn't be complicated at all.

Tristan, who runs the Natural Navigation school, believes using the night sky to navigate is much quicker and easier than using a compass.

'I put together a lot of expeditions when I was younger and they usually ended up being big and ambitious,' he says. *'Then I discovered that a small journey, using nature to navigate, is just as challenging as a long one using electronics – and is, strangely, more fun.*

'if you're using a compass or GPS, the stars are really useful as a gross-error check'

'It's also a lot cheaper, which helps when you're young. It sounds crazy, but you can have as much fun crossing a wood for an hour using natural navigation as you can on an expedition that lasts a few days.'

The key skill, according to Tristan, is being able to find Polaris, the North Star.

'You can learn to find the North Star in under a minute,' he says, *'and then it only takes a few seconds to use simple navigation techniques.'*

Learning to navigate by the stars is a useful backup skill, especially if you're relying on technology at night: *'If your compass or GPS breaks, lets you down or disappears for some reason, you have a good alternative.*

'Even if you are using a compass or GPS, the stars are really useful as a gross-error check; they can let you know something's not right before the kit does. For example, if you're meant to be walking west and you spot the North Star on your left, it's probably time to pause and work out what's going on.

'It's also a really good skill for checking your kit is working before setting off. If the North Star and your compass disagree badly, it's definitely time to worry about the compass.'

He admits there is a rookie error to be aware of when first using the stars as your guide: *'All navigation works best if you pick a spot to aim for. Whether you're using a GPS, map, compass or the stars, it is best to choose* something in the landscape as your target. If you want to walk north, find something at ground level below the North Star to aim for.

'The key skill is being able to find the North Star'

'The mistake some people make is to try to walk towards the stars themselves – they end up wandering around with their heads tipped up, bumping into things and tripping over.'

Being able to navigate by the stars is a fast and reliable way to get a sense of direction when you are walking outdoors at night. *'The stars never break or run out of batteries,'* Tristan adds. *'In every expedition group there is usually someone who knows how to find their way by using the stars – and it's great if that someone is you.'*

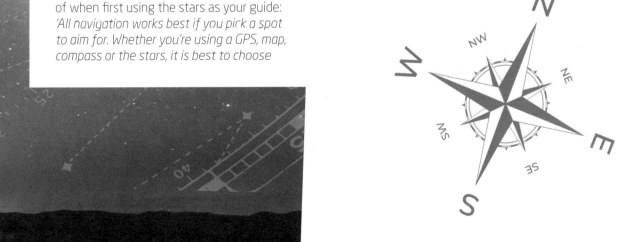

Star navigation for beginners

» Find the North Star

The easiest way to find Polaris, or the North Star, is by finding the Plough, an easy-to-identify group of seven stars. This group is known as the Big Dipper to Americans and is sometimes nicknamed 'the saucepan'.

Next you need to find the pointer stars – these are the two stars that a liquid would run off if you tipped up the saucepan. The North Star will always be five times the distance between these two pointers in the direction they point (away from the pan). True north lies directly under this star.

It's important to remember that the Plough rotates anti-clockwise about the North Star, so it will sometimes appear on its side or even upside down. However, its relationship with the North Star never changes and it will always dependably point the way to it.

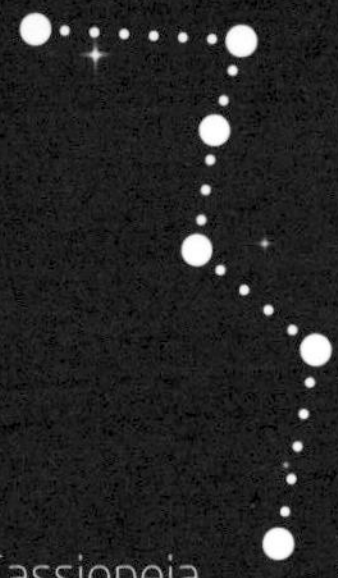

'The North Star is so important because it sits directly over the North Pole'

'The reason the North Star is so important for natural navigation is that it sits directly over the North Pole,' says Tristan. 'People often forget that whenever you are trying to find true north, you are actually trying to find the direction of the North Pole from wherever you are – even if you are only heading a few hundred metres on a gentle walk. "North" is still just an abbreviation for "towards the North Pole".'

Cassiopeia

Polaris (North Star)

» Check for Cassiopeia

The constellation Cassiopeia is also very helpful in finding the North Star. It will always be on the opposite side of the North Star from the Plough, and therefore often high in the sky when the Plough is low or obscured.

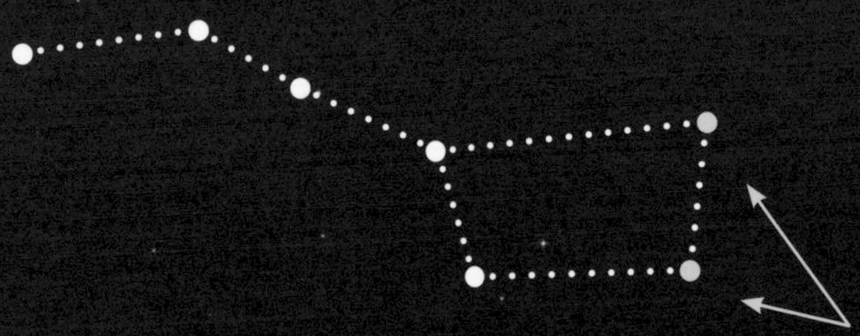

The Plough

Pointer stars

» Estimate your latitude

Wherever you are in the Northern Hemisphere, the North Star will be the same angle above the horizon as your latitude. This can be measured accurately using a sextant (pictured), but an estimate can be made using an outstretched fist.

An outstretched fist makes an angle of close to 10 degrees for most people. In under a minute, and with just your bare hands, you can find north and therefore estimate your latitude.

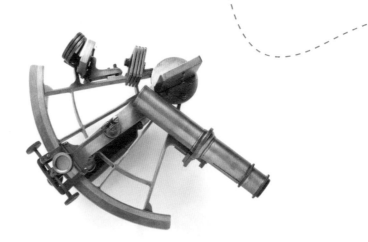

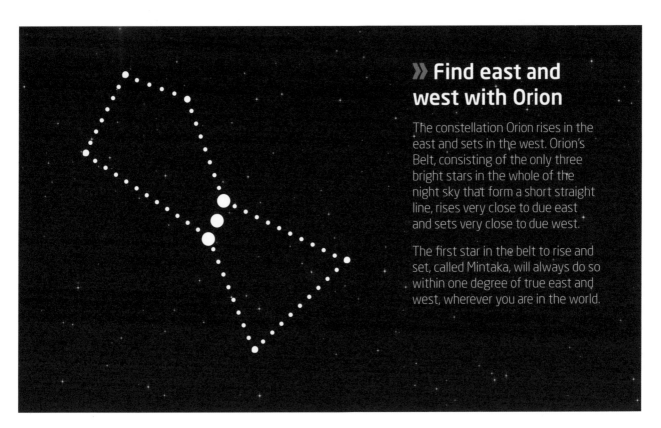

» Find east and west with Orion

The constellation Orion rises in the east and sets in the west. Orion's Belt, consisting of the only three bright stars in the whole of the night sky that form a short straight line, rises very close to due east and sets very close to due west.

The first star in the belt to rise and set, called Mintaka, will always do so within one degree of true east and west, wherever you are in the world.

Tristan has written lots of books and runs online courses on how to use the sun, moon, plants and animals to help you find your way on land, at sea and even in the city. Check out his website here. »

Photo: Matt Thomas

Aiming for the Olympics

England Champ **Ruth Mwandumba** reveals what it takes to pull the trigger in competitive rifle shooting.

Intrigued by the idea of a sport that doesn't rely on strength and fitness?

If the answer is 'yes' then competitive rifle shooting could be for you. Yet while it doesn't necessitate an athlete's physique it does require composure, exquisite fine-motor skills, superb hand-eye coordination and the ability to hold your nerve.

It's the absence of huff, puff and sweat that initially attracted 25-year-old England Champion Ruth Mwandumba. She was given the opportunity to try rifle shooting in CCF at St Mary's College in Liverpool.

'I wasn't into fitness or athletics and wasn't a sporty kid at school,' she says. *'Shooting was the first sport I was good at and it drew me in because it didn't require impressive fitness.'*

Although Ruth likes to work out to feel at her best in competitions, there are two attributes much higher on her priority list.

The first is balance (so she can cope with the long periods of standing), which she cultivates by doing yoga, using a balance board and trying to hold her body still while on top of dumbbells and foam rollers. The second is mental preparation: competitions are nail-bitingly tense so being able to hold your nerve and exercise immaculate self-control is essential.

'Shooting is a mental sport more than anything,' she explains. *'I like to read books on sports psychology but some of my fellow competitors use apps.'*

'It's great to be in a sport you're passionate about and where you have fun'

The mental technique Ruth favours, to help her stay calm while practising hitting targets 10, 25 or 50 metres away, is self talk.

'Every athlete has a process they go through before they take a shot,' she says. *'For me, I tell myself every single part of my process so that when it comes to the point of taking the shot, I know it's going to be a good one. I don't just think about my process, I say it to myself in my head.'*

Despite the intense tension of competitions, Ruth loves the sport for its friendly community.

'It's great to be in a sport you're passionate about and where you have fun and make great friends,' she says.

'I've been able to travel with it, too, so I've made many international friends. Everyone is so welcoming in the shooting community and very helpful – especially when you first start – which I love.'

Ruth fits her training around studying for a PHD in epidemiology (she's working towards a career researching infectious diseases) at the University of Manchester, and her part-time job.

'I have to make sure I'm on top of my organisational skills and plan everything to a tee so I can shoot well and still maintain the other elements of my life. I've always known how far I want to go in the sport and, because I remind myself of that, I find ways to balance everything.'

Her long-term goal is to compete at the Olympics.

First, though, she'll have to pit herself against the shooting elite in major championships including the European Championships, World Championships and the European Games. Achieving the title of England Champion in her first season of competitive shooting was an incredibly encouraging start.

'I don't think even I believed it when it happened. I was new to the sport at the time and I don't think it fully hit me when I got that title. I can definitely say I am glad to have it – and that I have it for life now.'

Want to give it a go? Ruth says:

1. Ask a lot of questions and make enquiries. When I realised I had a natural knack for shooting I did a lot of digging. Some cadets don't realise how far you can go and that it's an Olympic sport. Ask someone higher up in the organisation the routes you can take to develop your interest.

2. Listen to every word your instructor gives you and try to apply it. A lot of cadets are just so excited about trying a new activity they forget to listen. The smallest details from your instructor, whether that's how to breathe or pull the trigger, will make your shot better.

3. Never believe it's too late: I didn't start competing competitively until I was 22. In this sport you can still shoot in the Olympics in your 50s and 60s.

SHARP SHOOTERS

Meet three cadets with a passion for rifles.

» Sophie Hodge
Wellington College CCF

Sophie, 16, shoots .22 and 7.62 calibre rifles in the prone position and enjoys the multiple challenges the sport throws at her.

'Not only do you have to have good stamina and concentration, you also have to master the art of multitasking and prevent yourself from getting distracted,' she says. *'For instance, you have to watch the direction, angle and speed of the wind, and change your sights accordingly. It all takes quick thinking.'*

Sophie has already made an impressive debut in the target rifle shooting world. In 2019 she made it to the George's Final at The Imperial Meeting, then in 2020 she competed in the Queen's Final – the Queen's Prize is the premier award for the Meeting's top shot.

Having taken up shooting at 13 years old, Sophie thinks it's

'You learn a lot about yourself: shooting highlights your vulnerabilities'

important to experiment, ask questions and do plenty of practise in the early days:

'You shouldn't feel intimidated when other people who have been shooting for the same amount of time improve faster than you. It took me about a year to really get to grips with shooting, and that was with consistent training. Everyone else in my year group had improved rapidly, and I was getting disheartened. Although this was mentally challenging, I just had to push through and not focus on other people.

'You learn a lot about yourself: shooting highlights your vulnerabilities, but it also helps you work through them and turn weaknesses into strengths.'

Sophie particularly enjoys the social side of the sport and says: *'You compete with people of all ages which leads to more healthy competition. There have been many occasions where more skilled shooters have offered me advice when something has gone wrong and that creates a brilliant feeling of community.'*

Bullet points

'Don't stress. Shooting is more a sport of the mind than one of the body. If your mind isn't in the right place, that bullet won't hit the right place. You need to be resilient and that takes time. Let yourself go through the motions: acknowledge the fact that a bad score might be frustrating – then move on.'

To Inspire To Achieve

» **Toby Cubitt**
Gresham's School CCF

Toby, 18, specialises in small and full-bore target rifle shooting and has been selected for the Great Britain Long Range Squad (the Palma squad) who'll take part in the 2023 World Championships in South Africa.

Photo: Gresham's School

'An initial squad of 50 has been selected and I'm hugely honoured to be one of them,' he says. 'I'm the youngest in the squad and have been given the opportunity to train with some of the best shots in the entire world. I would love to be a member of the final GB Palma team.'

Toby was also selected for the GBU19 rifle team and the British Cadet Rifle Team (Athelings), but respective 2020 tours of South Africa and Canada had to be cancelled due to Covid-19. In the meantime, he continues to compete in as many events as he can, including the National Rifle Association's annual Imperial Meeting at Bisley.

'The Imperial Meeting is the best shooting event in the sport's calendar,' he says. 'Every year that I go, it gets more and more exciting and I meet new people with the same interest.'

Bullet points

'You have to have commitment, determination and be enthusiastic about the sport. Listen to those who are more experienced and learn from your mistakes. There's always room for improvement, so strive to be the best you can be.'

Toby encourages other cadets to give shooting a go and says: 'It is one of the few sports where males and females compete at the same level.

'Army Cadets offers a great route into shooting because the support and infrastructure are already in place. Tours I've been selected for over the past couple of years have mostly been only available to serving cadets.'

» **Charlie Crosby**
Wellington College CCF

Charlie, 16, took up shooting at the age of 11 and competed in his first National Rifle Association Imperial Meeting when he was 15.

'Against all expectations I made it to the Queen's Final,' he says. 'It turns out I was the youngest finalist in 136 years. I am very proud to have been placed in the top 200 of the Grande Aggregate in both the Imperials I've attended.'

Charlie is currently in the Athelings team and, if he shoots well enough this summer, would like to make it onto the GBU19 rifle team.

'I'd really like to go to a university with a strong shooting team and/or obtain sponsorship to allow me to continue to keep going with the sport once I leave school,' he says. 'Being selected for the GB Rifle Team is my ultimate goal.'

Bullet point

'Learn to read the wind.'

Charlie's regular schedule involves training three times a week and attending a week-long Easter camp each year. He particularly loves long-range shooting and recommends other cadets give it a go.

'The instant I pull the trigger it feels like the only things that exist are me, the gun and the target

'Those taking up the sport may find they have a natural talent for it and shoot pretty well from the start but, if not, they shouldn't be put off as practise really does improve your skill.'

Seize the
SLEIGH

Bobsleigh is one of the most dangerous and thrilling of all the winter sports. We spoke to three athletes from BBSA (British Bobsleigh and Skeleton Association) to find out what it's like.

Captain Jo Ellett loading

To Inspire To Achieve

There can be few sensations on Earth that equal a run in a bobsleigh. Squeezed into a steel pod, competitors negotiate a series of wickedly steep bends as they plunge down a course of glazed ice at breakneck speed. They hit the biggest bends at more than 80mph and 5G – five times the force of gravity. Meet the athletes experiencing the thrills and spills.

» Éire Rowland-Evans

One student who knows all about the exhilaration of this high-octane sport is 18-year-old Éire Rowland-Evans, who is part of the BBSA crew.

'My first time on ice was mesmerising,' says Éire, who was the former Lord Lieutenant's Cadet for ACF Gloucestershire. *'I instantly clicked with the speed and thrill of the adrenaline sport and have never looked back.'*

Bobsleigh, of course, is not without its dangers (last year Éire broke her collarbone while competing) and the likes of a helmet, burns vest and ice spikes are mandatory.

'When you are the pilot of the sled you also need to memorise the track,' she explains. *'Every bobsleigh track is completely different, so you need to study all the corners very precisely in order to slide fast and safe. One wrong move and you could crash.*

'You also need to pay attention to when you breathe on a bobsleigh corner: if you breathe at the wrong time, the G-force could break one of your ribs or cause other damage. A pilot must consider all this while sliding solo at anything between 80-120kph.'

'If you breathe at the wrong time, the G-force could break one of your ribs'

Éire enjoyed plenty of sporting opportunities while at school and with the ACF. At 16 she was the youngest England U18 tug of war captain and she is also National ACF record holder for both 200m sprint and 100m backstroke in swimming. All this stood her in excellent stead for the gruelling selection process to get into Britain's bobsleigh youth squad.

Now in the senior squad, the Swansea University student's short-term goals are to represent GB at European and World Cup races, but her big ambition is to represent Team GB at senior level in the 2026 Winter Olympics in Italy. She also hopes to get into Sandhurst and join the British Army bobsleigh team.

» Captain Jo Ellett

Jo represented the British Army bobsleigh team for four seasons before stepping onto the international circuit.

She began as a brakewoman but was quickly moved to the front seat and has taken on pilot duties ever since. Off the track, she manages the team, administration and finances, but on the track it's quite a different story.

'Your role is to get a 170+kg sled from the top to the bottom of the mountain as quickly as possible,' says Jo. *'That comes with a lot of responsibility because when you are in a two-man/woman bobsleigh you have another person's life in your hands.'*

Jo, who is Operations Officer at 1 Royal School of Military Engineering, has fond memories of trying out new sports and activities as a cadet at City of London and North East Sector ACF. Her advice to other cadets is:

'Believe in yourself and you can achieve great things. Grab opportunities when they present themselves, otherwise you'll be the one to miss out. I never even dreamed of putting on a GB tracksuit but I put myself forward for the trials. Now I represent my country in an amazing sport.'

Jo is grateful for the encouragement the Army has given her and she's also worn the colours of the Corps of Royal Engineers in athletics, rugby and football.

'I never even dreamed of putting on a GB tracksuit but I put myself forward for the trials. Now I represent my country in an amazing sport'

She encourages cadets with an interest in sport to take advantage of opportunities like STEM camps.

'STEM is prevalent throughout bobsleigh: from understanding the mechanics of a sled and how it drives, the changing ice conditions and choice of runners, through to the finances of training and competing.'

'You might crash at 90mph but you still have to go back to the top and do it again'

» Lance Sergeant Lamin Deen

Lamin is a double Olympian who competed in bobsleigh at both the Winter Games in Russia (2014) and South Korea (2018). According to Lamin, hours of preparation – both physical and mental – are needed in the run up to every race.

'Before you even get on the ice you will have already rehearsed the run 30 or 40 times,' he says. *'In the minutes before you go down the hill you'll be going over it in your mind: the steers you'll do, trying to recreate the pressure in the ropes you'll be pulling and the position of your body when you make that turn – you could be 15 feet in the air at 80mph.'*

A sergeant in the Grenadier Guards, Lamin didn't set out to be an Olympian; he only got into professional sport through the Army.

'There's no way on Earth I'd have had the opportunity to do it otherwise,' he says. *'I've been a full-time athlete since 2012, doing nothing but sport. There is no other organisation that'll let you do that (even the Air Force and Navy aren't as kind to their sport personnel) and push you all the way.*

'After the last Olympic Games I was going to retire and it was part order, I think (in a nice way), when I was told: "We think you should carry on because we know your potential." With that kind of support and literally the whole Army behind you, it's hard not to be successful.'

Lamin believes the resilience and teamwork learnt in the Army are great assets for a professional bobsleigh athlete.

'You've got to be 100 per cent robust and have good camaraderie,' he says. *'In a practice run you might crash at 90mph but you still have to go back to the top and do it again. That takes a lot. It's like having a car crash, getting out and jumping into a different car and carrying on. And it's not only yourself you have to think about: you have to motivate, encourage and nurture the other guys to do the same.'*

Lamin encourages cadets to try sports they may not have thought about doing and says: *'See what you like and give it a go. I never had any dreams of competing at bobsleigh. I used to love the film* Cool Runnings *and the next thing I know I'm seeing the people who were in the movie. It was an opportunity I was given and I went for it.'*

British beach
ADVENTURES

From stand-up paddleboarding to surfing, there are some thrilling board sports to take British staycations to the next-level. Here's what you need to know.

To Inspire To Achieve

Bodyboarding

Basics

Bodyboarding is the art of riding unbroken waves while prone (lying down) or dropknee (half standing).

It's a watersport about speed, tricks and catching waves – like shorebreaks – that aren't easily ridden on stand-up surfboards.

Getting started

Bodyboarding at advanced level is a highly technical sport which includes acrobatic manoeuvres.

Beginners can have a lot of fun hiring a board and playing in the surf, but taking a lesson will enhance the experience and help you feel comfortable in the water.

You'll need

A bodyboard with a leash, and a wetsuit (or just swimwear and a rash vest in late summer). These layers will keep you warm, protect against sunburn and prevent rubbing. Extra kit includes fins and fin socks.

» Beginner tips

- Pay attention to how the board reacts to the different phases of each ride and how you adjust your body – this will help improve your skills.

- Stay centred on the board and with your chest raised as you ride to the shore. Move further forward for added speed.

- Only bodyboard at a lifeguarded beach.

» Cost

The cost of bodyboarding tuition depends on group size and the length of the lesson, but typically starts at £15 per person for an hour.

Board prices begin at £30. Don't buy a cheap board which will cause environmental damage when it inevitably breaks. You'll get much better value from a hired board of higher quality which will get used again by someone else. Hire ranges from £5-£20 per day.

Army Cadet National Ambassador Jordan Wylie says:

'I love being on the water; it's certainly my happy place. There's a feelgood factor you get from being on the ocean you can't find anywhere else.

'Watersports are great for body and mind. They can help build endurance, muscle strength and cardiovascular fitness. My favourite sports on or in the water are stand-up paddleboarding, rowing and swimming.

'If you're planning on heading to the beach with your board just make sure safety comes above everything else. Familiarise yourself with wind and tides and, most importantly, if in doubt don't go out.'

Stand-up paddleboarding

Basics

Stand-up paddleboarding (also known as SUP) is a versatile watersport which can be enjoyed in the sea or on rivers, lakes and canals. It's brilliant for beginners of all ages and abilities.

You stand or kneel on a large, sturdy board and move through the water using a paddle. The tough part is keeping your balance while standing on the board.

Getting started

To be up on the board as quickly and safely as possible, book SUP lessons. Most teachers will begin a lesson by asking you to kneel on the board in the water then, once you've found your balance, to plunge the paddle into the water and gently start to paddle. This will give you a chance to practise your paddle action with more stability than when standing up. Once you've conquered that you can move on to paddling while standing.

You'll need

A board, paddle, safety leash and life jacket. If you're paddling in winter or in colder climates you may consider a wetsuit or drysuit.

» Beginner tips

- It's best to start on a thick and wide all-round SUP that's easy to balance on in both flat and choppy waters.

- Stand up straight and look ahead for maximum stability.

- Investing in a pair of water shoes can help avoid sore feet, protect them from the sun and provide extra grip to help you stay upright on the board.

» Cost

SUP lessons typically start at around £25. Boards with paddles are available to buy in some mainstream supermarkets.

Renting equipment usually starts at £20 for a day's hire.

Surfing

Basics

Surfing remains the most popular board sport on British beaches.

Surfers paddle out before turning their board and waiting for an appropriate wave. They then paddle quickly and try to catch the wave and ride it. They jump from their belly to their feet (crouching or standing) and ride the wave towards the shore.

Getting started

Taking lessons with a certified teacher is essential in order to learn how to paddle efficiently, read the waves, get on your feet, and keep yourself – and others in the water – safe.

You'll need

A surfboard (with an ankle leash), wetsuit and surf wax (to help your feet grip the board). Additional extras include surf boots and hoods (in cold weather).

» Beginner tips

- Never surf alone at a beach that isn't lifeguarded, or in conditions in which you aren't comfortable. Check the forecast and online surfcams before going to the beach.

- Don't be disheartened if it takes a while to catch your first wave or to stand up – surfing takes practice.

- A surfboard's size and material are important, especially when learning. The bigger and more buoyant the board, the easier it is to balance.

» Cost

Surfing lessons typically start at around £35 but cost varies depending on group size and the length of the lesson.

Surf kit is often available for half-day hire – or for up to a week. Wetsuit day-hire ranges between £5-£15 and surfboard day-hire between £10-£30 depending on the board.

Beach safety
Know your flags

Red and yellow flags indicate the area is patrolled by lifeguards and the designated space between the flags is safe for swimming and bodyboarding.

Black and white chequered flags indicate the area is supervised by lifeguards and safe for use when undertaking watersports such as surfing and kayaking. Never swim or bodyboard in these areas.

A **red flag** indicates that conditions are dangerous and you must not enter the water under any circumstance. No swimming or watersports of any kind are permitted.

The **orange windsock flag** means there are offshore winds and you must not use inflatables in the water.

Only go in the sea at a lifeguarded beach. If you witness an accident, see someone in trouble or have any issues yourself, alert a lifeguard.

For more safety advice on beach sports, visit the RNLI website:

Army Cadets in
January 2021

» Cadets save woman's life

Thoughtful and quick-thinking action from two 16-year-old cadets saved a woman's life.

Lance Corporals Benjamin Duncalf (top) and Alfie Smith (bottom) of Cheshire ACF (accompanied by friends Ben Hobden and Harvey Slater) were at a supermarket in Cheshire when they encountered a woman in distress. The teenagers were so concerned for her welfare they followed her to the town's railway station, where their instincts proved correct as she attempted to put herself in danger.

The teenagers tried to persuade her to return to safety. When it became apparent she wouldn't, Lance Corporal Smith was able to physically move her out of harm's way. A train was approaching at the time, prompting the cadets to alert the driver of their presence using reflective clothing and the lights on their phones. They stayed with the woman until police arrived.

Lance Corporal Smith said: *'Being a cadet has taught me how to respond quickly using whatever you can find around you. When we saw the lady in distress we knew we had to help. My friends and I are happy we could intervene to prevent a tragedy.'*

Commandant Lieutenant Colonel Andy Webster of Cheshire ACF said: *'I am humbled by the outstanding bravery and selfless acts carried out by our cadets and couldn't be any more proud. Well done Lance Corporals Smith and Duncalf.'*

The cadets were featured for their bravery in their local *In Your Area* community news in January, and were nominated for a Praiseworthy First Aid Award.

» Praise for compassionate cadet

Bombardier (now Sergeant) Eilidh Dunwoodie of Harpenden ACF put her first-aid training into action when she found herself in the presence of a woman who had fallen at St Albans City railway station. Eilidh monitored the injured passenger and kept her warm until professional help arrived. Eilidh's quick thinking didn't go unnoticed: her actions were reported in the *Herts Advertiser* in January, and she received a bouquet of flowers as a token of gratitude from the station manager.

» Army Cadets Inspire

'Inspiring inclusion, respecting everyone' is the vision of **Army Cadets Inspire**, which works to make Army Cadets even more inclusive.

Its launch in January followed the amazing work done by the Step Change project in the previous 18 months. Lieutenant Colonel Darren Hughes (pictured), Army Cadets' first Diversity & Inclusivity Advisor, said: *'We have members from a wide range of backgrounds, so we need diversity and inclusivity to be the golden thread that runs through everything we do.'*

'We need diversity and inclusivity to be the golden thread that runs through everything we do'

Three pillars were established to act as focus points for Inspire activities: culture, education and recruitment.

'Regional advisors work closely with me to cascade key messaging, training opportunities, advice and guidance,' he said.

'There are opportunities for cadets and CFAVs to be involved in activities and information sessions, providing them with a greater understanding of why diversity and inclusion are important in our organisation.'

Members from across Army Cadets Inspire helped to create recruitment and information leaflets written in a number of different languages, from Arabic to Portuguese. These new leaflets, which are available to order from the Army Cadets webstore, help more young people learn about the organisation and how to join.

DIVERSITY & INCLUSIONS

CULTURE · EDUCATION · RECRUITMENT

INSPIRE

INSPIRING PEOPLE

Ready to be inspired? Meet Rebecca Stephens MBE who was the first British woman to climb the Seven Summits, learn about Colonel Lucy Giles' experiences smashing glass ceilings in the Army, and discover what some notable former cadets have gone on to achieve.

What I learnt ...

AS THE FIRST
BRITISH WOMAN
TO CLIMB EVEREST

Rebecca Stephens MBE was the first British woman to climb Everest and to scale the Seven Summits. She's trekked extensively in the Himalayas and Africa and, in 2001, crossed the Antarctic island of South Georgia in the footsteps of Sir Ernest Shackleton. She reveals what she learnt from her experiences.

Kami Tchering and Rebecca on Everest summit, 17 May 1993

» Starting the journey

I went to Everest in 1989 as a journalist commissioned to write an article answering the question, 'Why do climbers climb?'. I didn't know anything about mountains but had an interest in landscape, other cultures, exploration and adventure.

I wanted to know why people would risk so much to get to that highest point and, to answer that, I went up to the first camp on the northeast ridge. It blew me away. It made me feel amazing, vibrant and alive, and that's when I decided I wanted to go back.

» On top of the world

My main feeling on reaching the top [four years later in 1993] was one of disbelief. We had made one attempt on the summit and got to the high camp, but retreated from there and waited about a week for the weather to improve.

'The emotion was one of unbelievable shared joy'

I was the only one left in our team able to give it another crack because there were two Sherpas in a position to go with me. It was the eleventh hour, the forecast was bad, I was a relative newcomer – the leader of the expedition was down the mountain, not with us – so there were a million reasons not to climb that night. But we did climb and eventually found ourselves ten minutes from the summit with no obstacles in our way.

I had a smile across my face like the Cheshire Cat because it had seemed impossible. When we got to the top it was just the three of us there. It was stunning, and the Sherpas were equally thrilled as it was their first time, too. We were there for about five minutes, and the emotion was one of unbelievable shared joy. When I looked down at the glacier where I'd been (as a journalist) four years earlier it was an extraordinary feeling.

» The right path

When I reflect on my trip to Everest, getting to the top was only the cherry on the cake. I'm very, very happy that I did, but my memories aren't really about that. They're about the people I met: that's what enriched my life massively.

It was hard work, but it was made easier because I knew it was so right for me – it was my path. Don't let anyone tell you what your path is; you will find it. If the journey doesn't feel right for you, get on a different road.

Kami Tchering (left) and Ang Passang – the two Sherpas who climbed with Rebecca to the summit

» Challenges and doubts

Our chance of success of getting to the summit was low. People were saying we could go back up to the South Col (a sharp-edged col between Mount Everest and Lhotse) but that we wouldn't get any higher. Our doctor said we had about one in a hundred chance – and that was being optimistic!

There was one day when I didn't have the energy to get going, but after that day I found myself thinking, *What's in my control and what's out of my control?* And I did everything I could that was within my control. I had to know I'd done everything I could – and that's what motivated us to give it another shot.

Of course, judgement plays a strong part. If will is stronger than rationality you can make mistakes, and when you're somewhere like Everest that can be fatal.

» Inspiring leaders

Before I went to Everest, I interviewed Baron Hunt (John Hunt, who famously led the 1953 Everest expedition). We hit it off and I asked him to sign a copy of his book for me. Inside he wrote, *'To Rebecca, Good luck and mind you make it, John'.* I carried that mantra with me on the mountains, so when I was really struggling to take the next step I was reminded: *'Mind you make it!'.*

I got to know him later; he was an exemplary figure of how we can live our lives and contribute to the wider world. He went on to be the founding director of the Duke of Edinburgh's Award.

Harry Taylor, Dr Sandy Scott and Rebecca discussing whether Rebecca might climb back up to the South Col and make a bid for the summit

'If the journey doesn't feel right for you, get on a different road'

Kami Tchering, Ang Passang and Rebecca crossing the South Col to Camp 4 on return from the summit

» Altered perspective

When the reality of having completed the expedition eventually sank in, I realised the difference between doing something because you feel you should do it versus doing something because you truly love doing it. You've got a much better chance of achievement and fulfilment if you do something where you're flowing in the right direction rather than pushing uphill. I was very lucky to find that.

» Superficiality stripped away

The car we drive, the clothes we wear and our job title give us a position and identity in society, but that doesn't exist in the mountains.

We had a mix of people with us on the trip: from consultant doctors to out-of-work journalists (me!), but none of it mattered when we all had our eyes on getting to the top of the mountain. We were all in it together, and all we cared about was whether people were in the game or not, whether they were sapping energy or contributing towards the effort.

» Making mistakes

We shouldn't be shy of mistakes or experiments that fail. Isn't it better to fall forwards rather than backwards? Pushing boundaries and discovering what works and what doesn't helps you discover who you are. I've tried plenty of things that didn't work, yet, in doing that, I found what did work for me.

» Finding your 'mountain'

Take opportunities that come your way to discover what's important to you, what inspires and stretches you or adds purpose to your life. Listen to your inner voice and have the courage to take your chosen path.

There are times when it's a grind to get where you want to go, so don't be frightened of something that looks like it might stretch out for years in front of you. It's important to go that extra mile, to not give up halfway, and to realise how important it is to get on and work with others. And be disciplined – it's an underrated quality!

Go further

Watch Rebecca's talk for TEDxYouth@ISH here

What I learnt ...

SMASHING
the glass ceiling

Colonel Lucy Giles reveals what she's learnt as the first woman to be promoted to top Army roles traditionally held by men.

C olonel Lucy Giles RLC has smashed through a few glass ceilings during her near three-decade career.

She was the first female officer to command 47 Air Dispatch Squadron, facilitating operations in Afghanistan and Iraq. In 2015, she became the first woman in British history to be made New College Commander at the Royal Military Academy Sandhurst (RMAS). Then she broke the mould again when she became the first female President of the Army Officer Selection Board.

Although Lucy now has a carpet of shards beneath her boots, she's certainly not tiptoeing around the responsibilities that come with success, and shares some lessons she's learnt along with way.

Photo: Bar Murray Ker – RMAS

'Don't be afraid to challenge barriers - especially those you've put up for yourself'

» Don't be complacent

On becoming Commander of New College at RMAS, Lucy received an entry into Debrett's *People of Today* and won the 2016 inaugural Women in Defence 'Inspirational' and 'Woman of the Year' awards. She says:

'It's all very well smashing glass ceilings but you have to watch you don't get cut. You need to maintain your momentum when you get into your next job; you can never become complacent.'

» Pay it forward

Lucy believes it's important that people help those climbing the ladder behind them, which is why she became an ambassador for First Women UK, a Girl Guide Ambassador and joined the Girls' School Association teachers' mentoring programme.

'I have two children and like to be involved in youth organisations,' she says.

'I see the value of investing in young people, and I want to do everything I can to help – as a leader in the Army and as a role model. It's important to pull up people behind you.'

» Don't be afraid to challenge barriers

By the age of 25, Lucy was commanding 72 men on operations in Bosnia. She's served in over 20 countries including Iraq, Afghanistan and Northern Ireland, excelling in a field that's 90 per cent male. Her advice to young women is to challenge barriers – both internal and external.

'Young females are brought up in a world where the frame of reference tends to be masculine,' she says.

'If I could go back in time, I'd tell my younger self not to be put off by what you can't do, but to look at what you can do. Also not to be afraid to challenge barriers – especially those you've put up for yourself.'

» Be a good follower

During Lucy's career she's come to value 'followership' (a term coined by USA retired four-star general Colin Powell) as much as leadership.

'We're all followers within a military organisation. Even the Chief of the General Staff works for the Chief of the Defence Staff and the Secretary of State for Defence, who in turn works for the Prime Minister, who is ultimately responsible to the Queen.

'We all have to behave in a way that respects the role we play within our organisation. Being a good follower is as important as being a good leader.'

» Allow people to make mistakes

As Commander of New College at RMAS, and previously as instructor of junior majors at the Joint Services Command and Staff College, Lucy learnt the importance of creating an environment where people can learn from their mistakes.

'If you apply discipline straight away you create a culture where people are afraid to admit to their mistakes, which leads to shortcuts and being economical with the truth.'

'I'm a fan of unlocking potential and helping steer people in a different direction'

» Pressure hones leadership

Lucy has learnt that leadership is developed when the pressure is on.

'That pressure could be lack of sleep, being rationed, the pressure of time or even austere conditions. We deliberately create those at Sandhurst with the aim of constructing an environment where people have to make decisions under difficult circumstances. Leadership is only really practised when pressure is applied, otherwise it's just managing.'

» Build your team

Lucy believes building a solid team is crucial to success in any endeavour: she was one of the advisors helping England Football Manager Gareth Southgate hone his team prior to the UEFA Euro 2020.

'Having your team around you keeps your moral compass pointing in the right direction and towards the values instilled during training: courage, discipline, integrity, respect for others, selfless commitment and loyalty.'

» Avoid the word 'fail'

During her time as President of the Army Officer Selection Board she's come to dislike the word 'fail' when referring to candidates who don't get selected for officer training.

'I think it's misleading and unhelpful. Everybody has potential for something, and it might not be in the Army. I'm a fan of unlocking that potential and helping steer people in a different direction. Everybody has something to offer society and there are other ways to serve your country that don't involve being in the armed forces or on a sports pitch.'

Her advice to young people who are keen to pursue an Army officer career is to explore The Army Officer Scholarship Scheme.

'There will be some young people, still at school, who have their heart set on becoming an officer. They should be aware that the Army has a scheme to help support them through school and university. The Army Officer Scholarship Scheme (AOSS) is offered to high-quality students who have the potential to make excellent Army officers, particularly those who will be good ambassadors for the Army during their time at university or college.'

» GO FURTHER Scan here to find out more about The Army Officer Scholarship Scheme

Clockwise from far left: Lucy in No1 Dress uniform outside New College at the RMAS; on deployment in Iraq; with her children Jess and Alex at the Army Officer Selection Board, Westbury

Lucy's message to cadets:

'Putting on the uniform and experiencing some aspects of what we do in the Army is great, but what I hope you'll learn is the experience of working within a group, how to be selfless, and the sense of discipline we need to have when serving our country.'

Lucy's message to CFAVs:

'A huge thank you. The effort you put in to develop your people and give them unique experiences, allowing them to challenge themselves and bond as a team, is fantastic.'

From CADET to...

Cricket consultant, Army Officer Scholarship winner, astrophysics tutor and punk-rock mayor. Four former cadets share their stories.

From cadet to ...
Cricket consultant

» Summer Keightley

Aged 17, Summer was the first cadet to represent the British Army cricket team. She now works for Northamptonshire Recreational Cricket Board, delivering sports sessions at primary schools across the region. She became a CFAV in 2018 in order to give back to Army Cadets, which she credits for many of her achievements.

What inspired you to join Army Cadets?

I was 12 and my dad was an instructor and my brothers were cadets. I'd always said I'd never join, but they persuaded me to try it and I never looked back. I enjoyed drill and the sports the most. I was quite a shy person before I joined, but being a cadet definitely gave me more confidence.

What was it like representing the British Army in cricket?

I was the first cadet to represent the British Army in any sport and the youngest player in

'I was the first cadet to represent the British Army in any sport'

the cricket team. It was an amazing experience and great to hear stories from serving members of the armed forces.

Why did you become a CFAV?

My original plan was to join the Army but I injured myself playing cricket so couldn't follow that path.

I realised the next best thing was joining the ACF as an instructor and was happy to have the opportunity to give back to an organisation that helped me achieve so much.

The adult volunteers played a massive part in my development when I was a cadet. They believed in me when I didn't believe in myself, and pushed me to be the best version of myself – which got me to where I am today.

As a CFAV it's brilliant to watch the cadets develop. As I was a very shy child, it's inspiring to see the less confident cadets open up and become leaders.

Army Officer Scholarship winner

» Dillon Shah

Dillon (below right) being awarded the Cadet of the Year trophy in 2018

Last year, former cadet Dillon was awarded an Army Officer Scholarship which will support him through his studies and guarantee him a place at Royal Military Academy Sandhurst (RMAS) on completion of his degree. Dillon fought off tough competition to get one of around 60 places.

What inspired you to join Army Cadets?

I didn't know much about the armed forces until the Air Cadets hosted an assembly at my school when I was 14. It inspired me to do some research into the different cadet groups and I was excited by the range of activities offered by Army Cadets.

Why did you apply for the Army Officer Scholarship?

I've always been interested in computer science but knew I couldn't be someone who sat at a desk all day; I wanted something more active. I was looking at becoming an Army officer and came across cyber intelligence. At cadets we learnt the importance of intelligence

'I was looking at becoming an Army officer and came across cyber intelligence'

during fieldcraft exercises and how having a clear intelligence picture of a situation can minimise risk, so that inspired my choice.

When I was looking into the officer opportunities I came across the scholarship. My application was shortlisted for a scrutiny board and I was invited to attend the Army Officer Scholarship Board where I completed fitness and psychometric tests, had multiple interviews, wrote a current-affairs essay, did a planning exercise with presentation and scrutiny, carried out command tasks and completed an obstacle course.

How did your cadet training help prepare you?

My cadet skills helped most in the command tasks. We were in groups of six or seven and had to complete a number of challenging obstacles while carrying kit. You don't only have to prove your physical abilities, you also have to show your leadership skills. I think my experience made me stand out.

Any advice for cadets thinking about applying?

Things like this can seem daunting, especially if there's a long or complex path you have to follow, but I'd always advise just going for it – there's rarely much to lose.

From cadet to ...

Astrophysics tutor

» Raphael Oyelade

Seeing the stars clearly in the night sky for the first time during a DofE practice walk in the north Devon countryside was the moment that determined South East London cadet Raphael Oyelade's future career.

After leaving school he studied astrophysics and cosmology at Lancaster University and is now a tutor in the subjects. As well as pursuing his scientific interests, Raphael, who had polio as a child and uses crutches, completed the Gold Duke of Edinburgh's Award (DofE Award) and has given speeches about his achievements to five royal audiences, including the Duke of Edinburgh.

What was your experience of being in the Army Cadets?

I joined when I was in secondary school; I absolutely loved it and eventually became a sergeant major.

My physical disability meant my whole Army Cadets experience was completed on crutches – from drill to adventurous training. The organisation was very accommodating; if we were on an expedition there would always be a minibus following, ready to pick me up if I had to stop. It was never needed.

How did you meet the Duke of Edinburgh?

Expeditions with the Cadets planted the seed for undertaking

'I saw the Duke of Edinburgh getting up to collect my crutches. I was extremely humbled'

the DofE Award and I completed my Gold Award when I was at university. Soon after, one of the DofE team asked me to give a talk about my story at Buckingham Palace to Prince Edward and other donors. It went so well they asked me to do more, including a private dinner at Frogmore House, hosted by the Duke of Edinburgh.

I was incredibly nervous but he was hilarious and very kind. I had to give my speech in the middle of dinner and once I'd sat down someone kindly moved my crutches to the side of the room. When I needed to stand up to give my speech, I saw the Duke of Edinburgh getting up to collect my crutches and bring them to me. I was extremely humbled.

Which cadet skills do you draw on today?

As a cadet you learn to lead and put yourself out there. The confidence I gained being a cadet has led me to be the kind of person who always puts their hand up first.

Advice for cadets?

Make an attempt at everything and give it everything you've got. I often speak to former cadets and people who completed DofE and they, like me, discovered their passions by doing something they had feared or never tried before.

From cadet to ...

Punk-rock mayor

» Andy Wrintmore

Photo: Matt Cradsmith Photography

I n May 2021, former Army Cadet Andy Wrintmore, then aged 28, became Mayor of Frome in Somerset, making him the town's youngest born-and-bred person to hold the title.

Andy may not look like your average mayor – he's 6ft 9in tall, has a big beard and dresses entirely in black – but he's happily slipped into a role which sees him helping the local community and promoting his home town.

Previously he was the drummer in punk-rock band SickOnes, and, when not touring in the UK, Europe and America, worked in Frome's Co-op where he got to know everyone – and everyone knew him. It was while he was working in the store that someone suggested he stood for election on the local council and so he did, winning a seat in 2018.

Punk and politics might be an unusual combination, but it turns out that both his drumming and his work as a councillor have been informed by his time in Army Cadets.

Making the leap

It was a nudge from Andy's mum that got him to join Frome Platoon, part of Normandy Company, Somerset Army Cadets.

'There were a lot less guns than I thought there'd be, but it was a big adventure'

'I had two mates who I'd grown up with and they were thinking about joining. Well, you know what mums are like, they plot and scheme, and my mum told me my friends were going and one day asked, "Do you want to go too, Andy?".'

Although he knew nothing about "Army stuff", he liked watching Sylvester Stallone movies, playing video games and going out shooting with his dad, so he thought he might give it a go.

'There were a lot less guns than I thought there'd be,' he laughs, *'but it was a big adventure!'*

New friends

The dynamics of being in the platoon made a big impression on Andy. Some cadets were older and some younger, which meant he soon had friends in different year groups at school.

'We were all from different economic backgrounds: because Cadets was affordable for everyone, it was an extremely good way for people who wouldn't normally mix to be friends, and for kids who didn't have an affluent background to go somewhere and be equal.'

Andy (front row, far right) with Somerset Army Cadets' Silver Bugles Band

Drumming up enthusiasm

The Frome Platoon forms part of the Somerset Army Cadets' Silver Bugles Band, and this led to Andy's first introduction to playing a musical instrument.

'They gave me this snare drum one Thursday evening. I didn't know what to do with it!'

He remembers lining up on the range and being shown the correct doubles and sticking for songs. From then on, he never stopped drumming and he's never forgotten how it felt to play in that band.

'When all the drummers are doing the same sticking, when it's really uniform, there is something so cool about it.'

Musical memories

On one occasion the band were performing in front of a group of dignitaries at West Down camp on Salisbury Plain.

'We were facing out over the plain and we hit the last strike on that drum tattoo. We were so tight and well-rehearsed and we could hear it echoing over the plain.'

Being part of a team was important to Andy – even though his mates sometimes took the mickey. He remembers a performance at Montacute House in particular:

'We had some complicated choreography, with lots of crossing over and weaving between, and I got completely lost. I was flailing around somewhere in the middle and the bass drum came past and hit me in the head.'

> **'Cadets was a good way for kids who didn't have an affluent background to go somewhere and be equal'**

What did he learn?

'So much in the Cadets is "learning how to find it within yourself"', he says. He recalls going through some pretty tough times, like waking up at 3am at camp, soaking wet because his tent had come apart. On another occasion he was on an NCO training weekend, camping in a quarry. *'It was so, so cold! It was a horribly tough weekend – but I did get my lance corporal stripes.'*

Andy with his grandfather Ray Wrintmore, who served in the military

Discipline, respect, social skills and self-sufficiency are all skills that Andy has called upon in later life as a performer and then as Mayor of Frome.

'Performing as a cadet at town events, helping with Poppy Appeal collections and drinking tea with old ladies were my first taste of community work and it set me up well,' he says.

'The drumming is the most obvious gift, but the Cadets gave me multiple tools across multiple disciplines in life. You could say it made me a bit more of a Swiss Army Knife than when I went in!'

Army Cadets in
February 2021

» Bra-vellous cadet project

When Sally Orange (pictured, centre) went to Uganda to run a marathon, she took with her over 100 sports bras (donated by her Facebook followers) to share with women unable to acquire them.

This story inspired 17-year-old cadet Victoria Cranston of 16 Platoon Dunbar, Kohima Company, to start her own project. She encouraged fellow pupils at St George's School in Edinburgh to collect over 50 bras for local charity Smalls for All, which distributes underwear to people in need in Africa and the UK.

Sally said: *'I was incredibly impressed and pleased when Vicky contacted me to tell me one of my stories had inspired her. She asked if I would help her promote her project by sending a video.*

'Receiving a message from Vicky later telling me how successful it had been, and what joy and sense of purpose it had given her, filled me with great pride for her achievement.'

» Army Cadets projects go live

The new Army Cadets website – bang up to date with news, training materials, Army Cadet Magazine and more – went live in February.

The month also saw the launch of the **#NoFilter** recruitment and education campaign in Surrey to inform the public about Army Cadets. It was the first of its kind and a great success.

The campaign used radio, social media, online advertising, magazine advertorials and outdoor billboards, and would go on to be rolled out across other counties and regions from August onwards.

» International meet-up

Cadets and CFAVs from Northern Ireland and Canada came together for a virtual training session in February.

Talks, training and presentations were accompanied by a quiz and themed chatrooms where cadets could get to know each other.

During the weekend, Irish cadets and CFAVs got an insight into how their Canadian counterparts build and maintain shelters and equipment in extreme temperatures, while cadets from Northern Ireland shared their tactical knowledge.

On the Saturday evening, participants were joined by Deputy Commander Cadets Brigadier Stuart Williams, OBE, who said: *'Seeing the inspirational cadets from Canada and Northern Ireland reinforces how we provide incredible opportunities and set people up for lifelong success.'*

Cadets were also treated to a virtual visit from Army Cadets National Ambassador Sally Orange who spoke about her cold-climate expeditions.

» Silver success

Cadet Sergeant Will Kelly (pictured above left) of B Company's Selby detachment, Yorkshire (North and West) ACF, scooped a Silver iDEA (Inspiring Digital Enterprise Award) award.

County STEM Officer, Second Lieutenant Scott Baker, was extremely proud of Will's achievement and said: *'Cadet Sgt Kelly has stepped up his digital enterprise training by becoming the first cadet in the county to complete the Silver iDEA Award. This is currently the highest level available to cadets and is a great addition to his CV.'*

» Treats for NHS workers

Cadet Emily McMullan (pictured above right) showed her gratitude to frontline NHS staff at Nightingale Whiteabbey Hospital by baking them Valentine's Day goodies.

Due to a childhood diagnosis of scoliosis, Emily had first-hand experience of being cared for by the NHS and, during difficult times, she turned to baking as a distraction from the condition – even when she had to wear a full back-brace while cooking.

Emily's mum Karen was a medical receptionist at the hospital and, with her colleagues, was part of the NHS's response to the pandemic. Detachment Commander SSI Joanne McMaster of Glengormley Detachment in Northern Ireland said: *'Emily went the extra mile to help NHS staff and vulnerable people in her area.'*

WELLBEING

Nurturing our mental health is just as important as taking care of our physical health. Discover some tips to help you look after yourself (and your friends), and find inspiration in others' experiences.

All in the mind

Adventurer and Army Cadets National Ambassador **Sally Orange** is a mental health champion. She reveals how tough times led to achievements she never thought possible.

Sally running a marathon in the London Eye during the pandemic

100

'I've battled with my mental health since 2004,' says the adventurer, endurance runner, mental health champion and Army Cadets first female National Ambassador.

As a result, Sally is a passionate advocate for removing the stigma around mental ill health, suggesting we should talk about it in the same way we do the common cold.

'We all get colds every now and again. Sometimes it gets worse and turns into the flu. In extreme cases it may develop into pneumonia. But, on the whole, you don't feel great, you battle on or, if you can't cope, you take time off. Then you bounce back. It's exactly the same with mental fitness.'

Sally uses the term 'mental fitness' rather than 'mental health' and says: 'I'm a qualified physiotherapist so I've always been conscious of keeping on top of physical fitness – and physical and mental fitness are comparable.

'Imagine injuring your ankle. For some it will be a one-off event: it's painful, they get treatment, it gets better. But for others there will always be a weakness in that ankle. The issue may reoccur and it may change how they partake in activities. Mental fitness works in the same way and we need to keep our minds active and nourished in order to flourish.'

» Hiding it

'I managed to hide my struggles for a long time - until fairly recently mental ill health wasn't talked about. Then, in 2013, I had a life-changing episode which led to me being under the care of the mental health crisis team.'

However, even that didn't lead Sally to feel she could share what she was going through. An Army Reservist at the time, if she wasn't feeling mentally well and should have been going on a training weekend, she simply didn't go – without telling anyone the real reason why.

» Breaking the stigma

Part of the reason Sally felt she needed to keep quiet about her struggle was the stigma that, historically, surrounded mental ill health.

'I was on and off medication from 2004, but since 2013 I've been on it constantly; my diagnosis of clinical depression is due to a chemical imbalance in the brain and medication helps make my life so much better. Yet I battled for years because of the stigma of being on medication and was even told, years ago, I wouldn't get a job because of it.

'I managed to hide my struggles for a long time'

'If you're diabetic, you need insulin to top up what your body needs and this is the same. It's like saying to a diabetic: "If you're taking insulin we won't employ you."'

Thankfully there is more support available now, and more open conversation about mental health.

Sally finally started talking about the tough time she had been going through when she was selected to represent the UK in the 2016 Invictus Games – a competition open to individuals who've experienced life-changing or life-threatening illnesses or injuries. When asked why she was competing, she found herself explaining: 'Not all injuries are visible.'

'People started to tell her she was completely nuts. "So I did a marathon in a nut costume"'

» Racing forward

Sally is perhaps most well-known for holding multiple Guinness World Records™ for her epic marathons, which have been a challenge in a number of ways.

'It took 24 years from when I first wanted to do a marathon to actually taking it on because I was full of self-doubt and lacked self-esteem,' she says.

However, with the support of others and through goal-setting, she was able to run her first marathon – dressed as a superhero.

'When I crossed the finish line I truly felt like a superhero because I'd achieved something that, for so long, felt unattainable. And I managed to get the Guinness World Records™ title for the Fastest Marathon in Superhero Costume.'

Sally caught the marathon bug and wanted to do it all over again. She'd raised a large amount of money the first time and knew she needed to up the stakes if she were to do it again.

'I decided to do my next one dressed as an orange (because of my surname), and

got the Guinness World Records™ title of Fastest Marathon Dressed as a Fruit. It was so much fun and it made people smile.

'It opened up conversations about my fundraising for military charities that support mental health, and I found others would then open up to me about their own struggles.'

She decided to go global and eventually became the only person in the world to run a marathon on every continent while dressed as a piece of fruit.

» Memorable moments

'I met Prince Harry when I was dressed as a strawberry. He asked, "Why are you dressed as a tomato?"'

Then people started to tell her she was completely nuts because of all her fruity marathons. *'So I decided to run a marathon in a nut costume. One of my proudest moments was seeing the message pinned to my costume displayed in the Guinness World Records™ book. It said "Nuts about mental health? … together we can crack it!" To date I have achieved ten Guinness World Records™.'*

To Inspire To Achieve

» Locked down

During the pandemic, Sally ran a marathon in the iconic London Eye to symbolise the ups and downs the situation was having on the nation's mental health. She was isolated in a bubble and could only see people through a screen as she ran on a wheel that kept turning.

'Six days later, on World Mental Health Day, I went down a mine to run the marathon we called Beneath the Surface [Army Cadets' Guinness World Records™ achievement last October]. *It represented how we never know what's going on beneath the surface of someone else's mind.'*

How does Sally keep up her motivation for these feats of endurance?

'I look to others, to my friends who have been physically injured and gone on to achieve great things.

'I also remember my lowest point in 2013 and that I got through it, so I can get through this – my legs will be fine again in a few days! You also have to be passionate about the cause you are doing it for because that keeps you going as well.'

She is also a firm believer in setting achievable goals. *'My latest challenge was 100 miles of the NHS Nightingale Hospital. I did one mile a day in its vicinity for 100 days. Doing something little and often can lead to great things and make a huge difference.'*

» Next steps

'I still have ups and downs – my diagnosis is a recurrent disorder – but by talking about it I hope others will realise it's completely okay.

'We all deal with low periods to different degrees. I now use an app called Stay Alive where I store lovely photos of my nieces and nephews – a reminder that there's good in life even if you can't see it in the moment.'

Does she have more marathons on the horizon?

'I've been bananas, I've been nuts ... next I'm going to be crackers. I've got a cracker outfit I'm waiting to use for a future marathon.'

Sally's wellbeing advice for cadets

- Get help early – the sooner you get support the easier it is, as a problem shared is a problem halved.

- Break things down into small goals. If you are feeling really low, that could be as simple as getting out of bed or having a shower.

- Have a duty of care to yourself. On aeroplanes we're told to put on our own oxygen mask before helping someone else, as it's not possible to assist others if you can't breathe. So look after yourself or you won't be of value to others. We talk about selfless commitment in Cadets, but YOU have to be part of that too. Treat yourself as you would a friend.

What's on your mind?

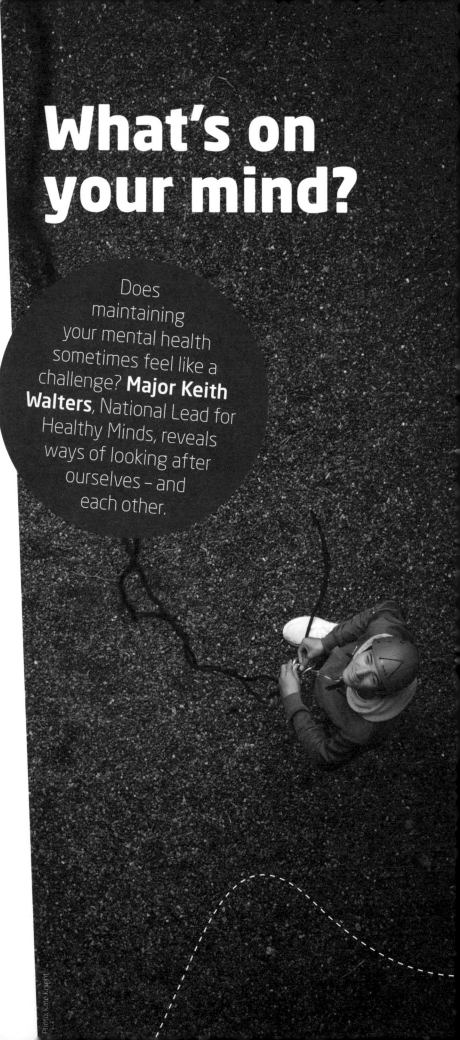

Does maintaining your mental health sometimes feel like a challenge? **Major Keith Walters**, National Lead for Healthy Minds, reveals ways of looking after ourselves – and each other.

Warning signs of poor mental health could include increased anxiety, struggling socially, acting out of character, and feeling withdrawn or quiet.

Support your friends by simply being there for them. Ask if they are okay. You don't have to have the answers; encourage them to talk to their detachment instructor or county Padre.

Great resources include the YoungMinds website, which has excellent tools including step-by-step guides to supporting your friends with their mental health. There's also Papyrus and Samaritans which have emergency helplines for those in desperate need. Mind also offers advice and support.

There's no shame in talking about your struggles. If you had a broken leg you would go to the doctor to get it fixed – it should be the same for mental health.

Useful organisations

www.youngminds.org.uk
www.papyrus.org.uk
www.samaritans.org
www.mind.org.uk

Photo: Kate Knight

Healthy Minds courses

Healthy Minds is a project designed to break down barriers, reduce stigma and promote mental health awareness within Army Cadets. We run various mental health courses aimed at cadets, CFAVs and staff cadets. We also plan to upload mental health support tools in the future.

The Healthy Minds Campaign was formally launched in September 2020 with the introduction of the Resilience in the Army Cadets online course (available to cadets and CFAVs via the Defence Learning Environment). This course was used to achieve our Guinness World Records™ title for most online participants on a mental health course in a 24-hour period.

WORKING WITH YOUNGMINDS

We've also collaborated with the UK's leading youth mental health charity, YoungMinds, to develop Healthy Minds Awareness courses which focus on supporting the mental health of our young people. These are available for people to book via the Cadet Forces Resource Centre.

In addition to the Awareness courses, our CFAVs have the opportunity to be trained to deliver the courses at their local level – this is the Healthy Minds Facilitators course which is run three times each year at CTC Frimley Park.

SUPPORT FOR CFAVS

We are also in the process of developing a Healthy Minds Awareness course focused on supporting the mental health of our CFAVs, as well as a programme for our staff cadets.

Photo: Kate Knight

Healthy Minds' five tips for good mental health:

1. **Connect with others** by spending time with family, friends and cadets at events like detachment nights, weekend activities and annual camp.

2. **Stay active** as increasing your heart rate releases positive endorphins. At Army Cadets you can take part in the Keeping Active syllabus, Adventurous Training, Fieldcraft, Expeditions and Drill.

3. **Learn** something new to enhance self-esteem. Try a new hobby or skills like kayaking, shooting, map reading or first aid with Army Cadets.

4. **Give** to others to improve your wellbeing. This could be through teamwork in Cadets or in your wider community.

5. **Take notice** of the world around you. Switch off your phone and see your surroundings. Connecting with nature and living in the moment can do wonders for mental wellbeing.

Books that INSPIRE US

Moving memoirs, fascinating history and inspiring stories motivate us and develop our resilience. We asked members of the Army Cadets family to reveal the books they've found useful.

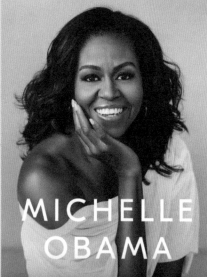

» *Becoming* by Michelle Obama

Chosen by Major Dionne Konstantinious, Officer Commanding 7 Coy GLSESACF and co-chair ACF BAME

I first skim-read *Becoming* in 2019 after I received it as a birthday present. However, during the first lockdown I reread the whole thing. I needed inspiration at a time when I was unable to plan and fully engage with my social norms.

It felt easy to connect with the author: a woman who hadn't settled for second best and who had created opportunities for her own success in her personal life, work and public duties.

At a time when I felt I was dealing with a disturbing backdrop of stress and uncertainty, I felt inspired by this book. It's a reminder that there is always hope and it's an encouraging read for any young woman looking for a role model. Michelle Obama demonstrates the importance of having someone to look up to – in particular, those who look like oneself.

I'm looking forward to the journey ahead and learning more about myself. No one gives you a rulebook when you first become a leader: you learn from those who have gone before you and those you lead. The book reminded me it's okay not to always have the answer.

Becoming is an easy read from a woman who speaks with exceptional intelligence and uses her platform to share positive messages of hope, encouragement and empowerment.

» Mindfulness: Finding Peace in a Frantic World by Mark Williams and Danny Penman

Chosen by Lieutenant Sophie Broyé RNR, Officer Commanding Royal Navy Section at Ryde School with Upper Chine

I was recommended *Mindfulness* by my friend and mentor Colonel Tim Boughton who is Head of Mental Health Engagement for the Army. It changed his life a few years ago when he realised he had PTSD.

Before I read the book, I knew next to nothing about mindfulness and was surprised how much I learnt and how much of it resonated with me.

It revealed I could retrain my mind to become my friend and not my enemy. It showed me how to become more compassionate and forgiving towards myself and those around me. Tim told me this book would change my life and that's exactly what happened!

It totally changed my path – especially during the pandemic. It introduced me to the world of meditation and mindfulness and I'm about to start an MBCT (Mindfulness Based Cognitive Therapy) course with the Oxford Mindfulness Centre to become a practitioner.

I'd recommend any CFAV to read it. Not only does it teach you patience, acceptance and, most importantly, living in the present moment, it also adds another dimension to your pedagogical tools, techniques and approach.

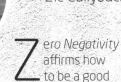

» Zero Negativity by Ant Middleton

Chosen by Amanda Roxborough, Colour Sergeant, 2ic Cullybackey Detachment, 1st (NI) Battalion ACF

Zero Negativity affirms how to be a good leader by looking for the strengths and weaknesses in yourself and getting to know who you really are. It also reflects on the importance of working as a team and understanding other people's strengths and weaknesses. Positive outcomes are achieved by inspiring others, remaining positive, removing yourself from negativity and not tolerating bullying.

It reminded me how CFAVs can make a positive contribution to the lives of cadets. Our motto is "Inspire to achieve" and I hope, by leading by example, we can help cadets leave the organisation as independent young people who will not only be successful in life but also help those less fortunate than themselves.

In many ways the book incorporates Army Cadets values: selfless commitment, teamwork, respect for others, loyalty, support, integrity, being honest with yourself and others, and discipline (doing things right and setting the right example).

It's a rereadable book and I'll be returning to it from time to time.

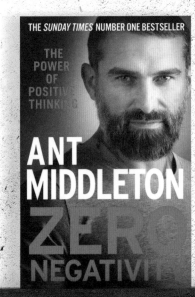

Books that
INSPIRE US

» Tomorrow Will Be A Good Day: My Autobiography by Captain Sir Tom Moore

Chosen by SSI Vicki Kirk, Detachment Commander of Northfield Gardens Detachment, A Company, Durham ACF

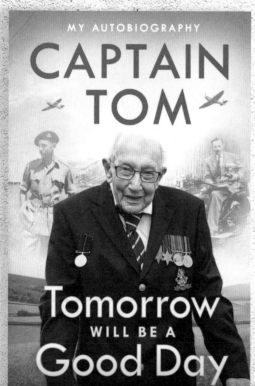

Tomorrow Will Be A Good Day gave me a lot of motivation and inspiration to find my get-up-and-go.

As a detachment commander, when face-to-face training was first suspended last year I kept cadets motivated and engaged with different activities and virtual parade nights. However, as the pandemic continued and the return to face-to-face training looked unlikely, I began to lose motivation and ended up feeling a bit fed up.

'This book gave me the will to do more and I think it will help others find the motivation to do more'

After reading Captain Tom's book about his health recovery and his mission to do laps of his garden [which raised over £32m for the NHS] I got my motivation back.

Tom was just a regular guy who had a normal childhood and served in the military. He was a *"quiet soul, living out his days peacefully"* until the world became interested in his story. As he said: *"It put a spring back in my step."*

This book gave me the will to do more and I think it will help others find the motivation to do more.

» Defeat into Victory by Field-Marshal Sir William Slim

Chosen by Steve Parker, the British Army's Command Sergeant Major student while attending United States Army Sergeants Major Academy in El Paso, Texas

Defeat into Victory is an especially precious book for me as it was gifted to me by my previous commander, Lieutenant General Sir Tyrone Richard Urch KBE. It was his own copy and his favourite book, and it came with a moving personal note.

I believe it's the best book on leadership: it covers the art and science of war, the interpersonal tact required to be a great leader, as well as lessons on the art of command, basic soldiering and leadership which are lacking in many other memoirs.

If you're a military history buff it's a must-read. It's a little slow at the start when things are going badly for the British Army, but things really accelerate once it switches to the offense action.

» From Pillar to Post: The Pearly Pellard Story by Pearl Brotherton

Chosen by Lieutenant Colonel Bryon Brotherton, former Commanding Officer of the Cadet Training Centre, Frimley Park

I typically read autobiographies: I find it fascinating how someone's early years set the trend for their life.

One autobiography that's extremely dear to me was written by my mother. It's called *From Pillar to Post: The Pearly Pellard Story* and is about her challenging childhood – some of which I knew nothing about.

I was on operations in Kosovo as a sergeant when I received it and I couldn't put it down. I was devastated to find out what her childhood had been like, but also full of admiration for her as a successful wife, mother and grandmother who hadn't let her background affect her negatively.

As a piper, I used her story as inspiration for the composition of a piece of music called *Piobaireachd*. The tune starts slowly to reflect the sad parts of her life, but then the tempo increases to mimic the positive and energetic times. A few years later I was fortunate enough to record her tune on an album.

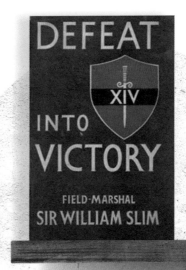

Army Cadets in
March 2021

» Highlanders' lockdown teaching course

CFAVs of 1st Battalion The Highlanders ACF held a national teaching course for 45 junior cadets during lockdown.

The course, conducted over three weekends in March via Zoom, taught cadets how to instruct their fellow cadets using lessons from the Army Proficiency Certificate (APC) syllabus.

The Junior Cadet Instructor Cadre (JCIC) is an integral part of 3-star training and designed to teach cadets how to instruct up to 1-star level in Drill and Turnout, Military Knowledge, Navigation, Skill at Arms and Fieldcraft.

In addition to the core elements of JCIC, there were presentations on leadership and talks from high-profile members of the organisation, and a welcoming address from Army Cadets National Honorary Colonel Lorraine Kelly CBE.

» Online inspiration

Major Chris Peacock's series of inspiring interviews with prominent leaders and Army Cadets National Ambassadors went live on the Army Cadets YouTube channel.

In the weekly series, interviewees such as Mark 'Billy' Billingham and Levison Wood reminisced about military experiences, discussed leadership and gave advice to young people. The episodes are still available to stream on the Army Cadets YouTube channel.

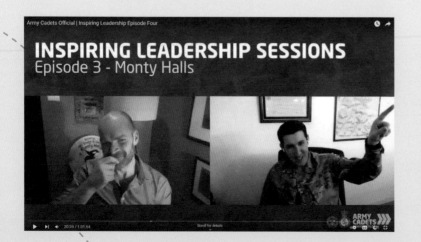

❯❯ International Women's Day

B Company of Yorkshire (North and West) ACF recognised the contribution of women to the organisation by spending International Women's Day celebrating its female admin officer and female PRO at HQ, and a significant number of female CFAVs in leadership roles across the detachments.

Four of its CFAVs have taken the first step toward becoming ACF officers: AUO Nette Studd of Selby Detachment (top left), AUO Kayla Oakey of Woodlesford Detachment (top right), former Cadet RSM now AUO Natalie Dixon of Lumley Detachment (bottom left) and AUO Charlotte Lowther of Fulford Detachment (bottom right).

Major Rory Romani, B Company's Officer Commanding, said: *'For all of our female cadets who are considering becoming CFAVs in the future, you have great role models.'*

Army Cadets National Ambassador Sally Orange received the Special Award in the Women In Defence UK Awards 2020.

MARCH IN MARCH

❯❯ Smashing march

A huge number of cadets and CFAVs joined in the Combat Stress challenge which involved walking ten miles during the month to help raise funds for life-changing mental-health treatment for veterans. Some walked ten miles in a day, some spread it across the month and others ran the whole distance.

The initial fundraising target of £120,000 was smashed: it came in at £140,000.

SKILL UP

Want to take your cyber and STEM skills to the next level, or develop your musical ability through Army Cadets? Find out how to do just that – and discover how cadets honed their skills during lockdown.

Photo: Kate Knight

The future is CYBER

How much do you know about the digital world and how it affects your life? **Captain Robb Bloomfield**, CyberFirst Project Officer for the Cadet CIS Training Team, reveals why cadets should take their cyber skills to the next level.

>> What does 'cyber' mean?

It implies a relationship with information technology and computer systems, but more recently it's tended to be used as shorthand for computer security.

>> How does this affect us as individuals?

Each of us creates and consumes a mind-boggling amount of data every day – mostly without thinking about what we're doing. We're a millisecond away from people on the other side of the planet; we live in a world where a hashtag can start a global movement. Almost everything we use has become digitised – and that data needs safeguarding.

It's not only those who work in IT who need cyber skills, however. It's important to have an understanding of how digital issues affect all areas of work, from marketing to law and finance.

» What is cyber warfare?

Those cliché scenes in films (ATMs failing to function and planes falling from the sky due to hacking) are exaggerated, even if they do have their origins in elements of real-life situations. The idea of using a computer virus to destroy whole systems is fairly outlandish. There are examples, but you can count them on one hand as they are very rare and extremely difficult to pull off.

'We live in a world where a hashtag can start a global movement'

Cyberspace *is* a domain of warfare, however, (something NATO recognised in 2016) and military operations do need to be protected from theft of information, sabotage and from preventing systems from functioning the way they are intended. It's important to show we have strong cyber defences and that we're not a worthwhile target.

» What's the deal with cyber attacks?

They are increasingly about money – certainly with WannaCry (which severely hit the NHS and businesses in 2017) there was a financial factor.

We should only be worried about our own information if we aren't taking day-to-day defences. It's not up to the military or the government to safeguard us. Cyber attacks spread because of vulnerabilities, so individuals who play their part by keeping systems up to date are actually contributing to the global defence picture.

For those considering a career in the military, cyber knowledge is as important as in any other workplace. And it's not just The Royal Signals who need to be experts. Just like in the civilian world, systems are increasingly being digitised and this affects everyone – from the Intelligence Corps using tech for reconnaissance, through to infanteers using tablets on the battlefield.

» Is cyber a career for geeks?

We want to discourage those stereotypes; there isn't a one-size-fits-all "cyber person". We need to continue tackling the under-representation of women in cyber and promote an environment that's welcoming, encouraging and inclusive.

There are a few skills and characteristics that are important, though. Because technology is constantly changing, you need to be adaptable, curious and willing to continually learn and develop. Everyone in cyber seems to end up doing a job that's slightly different from the one they applied for! Academic qualifications are useful but not essential, and many go out of date very quickly because there's such a fast pace of change.

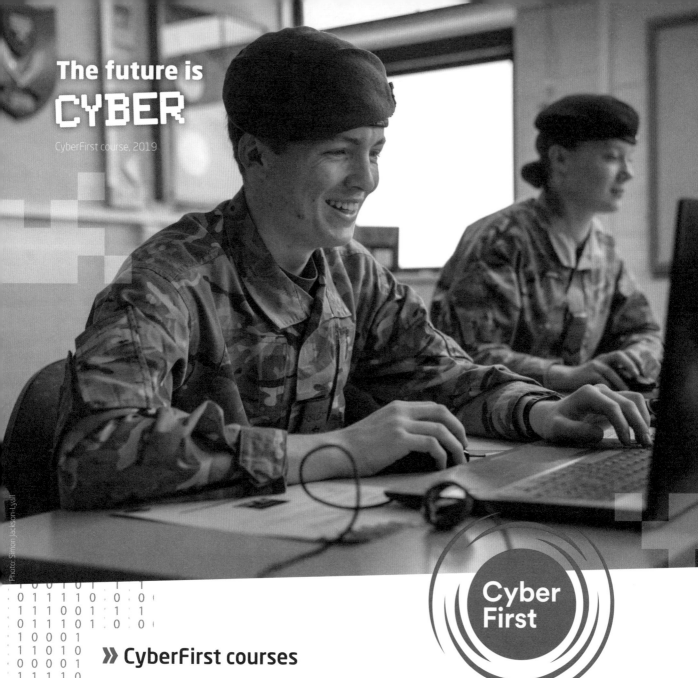

The future is
CYBER

CyberFirst course, 2019

Photo: Simon Jackson-Lyall

» CyberFirst courses

This is a free programme of opportunities put together by the NCSC (National Cyber Security Centre – part of GCHQ).

It provides a series of courses as well as bursary and apprenticeship schemes and access to competitions.

The first course, for junior cadets, is CyberFirst Adventurers. Over one day, cadets get a broad intro to cyber by doing data processing, open-source intelligence gathering, codebreaking and puzzle solving – showing how relevant cyber is to all kinds of disciplines. The course is delivered online via screen shares and virtual labs.

The second course is Defenders. This approved 4-star course is one week long and heavily focused on defence, including technical aspects such as security and privacy.

Cyber First

CyberFirst Adventurers is available to book via the Cadet Portal. Keep an eye on the portal for updates on Defender courses. Speak to your Detachment or School Instructor for more info.

To Inspire To Achieve

Cyber savvy: a beginner's guide

Use two-factor authentication whenever possible. Your email is the recovery address for Instagram, Facebook, Snapchat – in fact, every service you use, so if someone gains access they can hack into everything.

Check your digital footprint on a regular basis. Notice what you leave behind that people could see. The comments and shares you make, the things you obviously interact with: they all build a virtual picture of you which can be used for all kinds of purposes.

Check privacy and security settings, especially on new services and devices (which are almost certainly insecure by default). Your personal data is the cost of using a free service, so think about the information you're giving out.

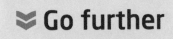

≽ Go further

❯ iDEA (Inspiring Digital Enterprise Award)

To learn about potential careers in coding and technology check out iDEA. It's free, accessible and recognised within the Army Cadets.

❯ BBC micro:bit

Those interested in hardware and programming should check this out. Many libraries carry micro:bit hardware so you can book it out and follow the projects at home.

❯ Raspberry Pi

This credit-card-sized affordable computer enables users to learn programming through fun, practical projects.

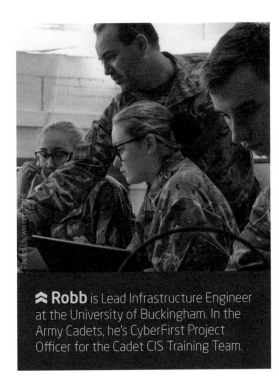

Photo: Crown copyright

≫ Robb is Lead Infrastructure Engineer at the University of Buckingham. In the Army Cadets, he's CyberFirst Project Officer for the Cadet CIS Training Team.

Banging the drum
for Army Cadets talent

Taking up an instrument is a brilliant way to learn something new while serving your detachment and community. **Colonel Mike Neville** reveals how to get started.

Pictures from parade at 2018 Warcop annual camp with Leicestershire, Northamptonshire and Rutland ACF

Photo: Kate Knight

To Inspire To Achieve

The thrilling spectacle of traditional military music played at a Remembrance Sunday event or on parade at annual camp is always a stirring sight. And the great news is that all cadets and CFAVs are welcome to be part of the impressive pageantry.

The opportunity to take up an instrument is open to everyone and, for those who show aptitude, it could even lead to a musical career.

Many military personnel who perform at events like the Changing of the Guard at Buckingham Palace and in prestigious concert halls throughout the world started their musical journey in Army Cadets.

Colonel Mike Neville, Commandant of Army Cadets Music (whose job it is to support the musical units of counties, battalions and sectors across the UK and Gibraltar) says: *'Music is a skill for life and a great way to make new friends. If you are very good, it's also possible to make a career out of it.'*

›› Prestigious performances

Army Cadets musicians take pride in playing for local communities, especially on Remembrance Sunday, and leading parades at annual camp and other events. There are international opportunities in which they can perform too:

'Our musicians have played all over Europe and in China,' says Mike. *'Each year, we take a group of senior musical cadets to Gibraltar where they perform at numerous events, including inside St Michael's Cave in the heart of the Rock. They also teach the local cadets.'*

›› Large choice of instruments

The spectrum of musical instruments cadets can take up is impressive. Bands revolve around brass instruments (trumpets, cornets, tubas), woodwind (flutes, saxophones, clarinets) and percussion (including a drum kit). Corps of Drums is made up of drums, bugles and flutes; Pipes and Drums consists of bagpipes and Highland

drums; and at camp, contemporary music is played by cadets on keyboards and guitars.

Mike stresses that cadets don't need to have a musical background to take up an instrument. They can visit their county music detachment and speak to the detachment commander if they are curious about exploring the opportunities.

'Music is a skill for life. If you are very good, it's possible to make a career out of it'

'The detachment commander will allow you to try different instruments or attend one of our camps,' says Mike. *'There's no need to be part of a recognised musical unit to attend, and all cadets are welcome.'*

›› Tailored training

Cadets can work towards Music 2-, 3- and 4-star awards and the training they receive at camps is tailored to their ability. They can also enrol for musical versions of BTEC at Level 1 and 2, and music qualifications can also be delivered through the Scottish Qualifications Authority.

'Some cadets attending our camps may have had private lessons or be learning an instrument at school, so they may already be very good musicians and will be placed in a section suited to their ability,' says Mike.

'The training is totally bespoke so if a Grade 8 trumpet player joins a band, they would play with the senior cadets, but be given extra band drill lessons to ensure they can fit into the marching band.'

Cadets can also use their musical abilities to pass the skill section of the Duke of Edinburgh's Award, as camps are recognized in the residential section of the Gold Award.

Photo: Dougie Johnston

Pass it on

Teaching music can be enormously rewarding for CFAVs, and music is a great way to raise the profile of Army Cadets in the community.

'Working towards teaching qualifications means you can pass on new skills and provide musical support at local events,' says Mike. 'A lot of cadet training is hidden away in cadet huts, Reserves centres or on camps, but music is a really visible part of Army Cadets.'

» Never too old to learn

CFAVs are welcome to get involved too. For those who may be nervous about taking up a new skill later in life, Mike has this advice:

'Just come along to our camp: you'll be among other beginners of all ages, and you'll make friends from across the country.'

As Detachment Commander in South East London ACF, Mike already had a musical background (he played guitar in a rock band as a teenager), but he decided to show his commitment and taught himself to play the flute. After setting up a Corps of Drums, he was offered the opportunity to become the National Training Officer for Army Cadet Music.

'We can teach old dogs new tricks,' he promises. *'I am always impressed by instructors, some in their sixties, who are willing to be a beginner and learn something new to help their cadets.'*

» Support is continuous

Training to become an instructor takes place at four week-long musical camps each year (two for bands and Corps of Drums and two for bagpipes and drums) held at Easter and in October half term.

'Regular instructors from the Drums Wing, Army School of Ceremonial, and Royal Corps of Army Music attend. They teach CFAVs and there's a course for beginners who want to learn more,' says Mike.

'At the end of the course, instructors are given a six-month development plan and are tested at the next camp. Once they are up to 2-star standard, they can attend a music version of the IIC/AIC to become an instructor.'

> ### 'Music is also the only area of Army Cadets life where a cadet can replace a Regular soldier at events'

Photo: Matthew Childs

» Homegrown success story

Mike thinks Army Cadets should be immensely proud that CFAVs are now filling teaching roles traditionally taken by the military.

He recently visited City of London and North East Sector Army Cadets (COLNES) where he was impressed by 15 cadets who proficiently played 2-star Corps of Drums tunes, and buglers who sounded the Advance.

'What I thought was especially noteworthy was that all the instructors had been trained in the ACF. There were no ex-Regular or Reserve musicians or drummers. In times past, bands and Corps of Drums were utterly reliant on such instructors. Now we take non-playing adults and train them on music camps.'

» Career openings

For cadets and CFAVs with ambitions to pursue music within an Army career, gaining qualifications with Army Cadets could leapfrog progression.

'All 4-star band cadets are entitled to an audition to join Royal Corps of Army Music, and cadets who pass 3-star Corps of Drums are given a certificate by the Senior Drum Major of the Army. This means if they join the Army, they are already up to the standard of a Class 2 drummer and need no further training.'

Music is also the only area of Army Cadets life where a cadet can replace a Regular soldier at events.

'A 14-year-old bugler or piper can be as good as a 24-year-old. When the community wants the calls played at Remembrance Sunday, the Army Cadets is often the organisation they ask, as there are less and less Regular and Reserve musicians to help them.'

As for those who want to travel, Pipes and Drums qualifications are internationally recognised so also provide CV-building opportunities.

Get involved

Email Mike: **355nevill@armymail.mod.uk** or SO2 Cadet Bands Tex Calton at **248calto@armymail.mod.uk** or contact Maj Ross Munro SO2 Cadet Pipes and Drums at **piping_drumming@armycadets.com**

An opportunity to find out more about the Green Hornet mini-drone with the Royal Artillery (RA) during Exercise STEM Challenge at Westdown Camp

What's the deal with STEM?

Not clued up on STEM? You should be. Science, Technology, Engineering and Mathematics are vital in the working world – now and in the future. **SMI Kate Dunscombe VR** explains why.

» What's STEM all about?

Science, Technology, Engineering and Mathematics (STEM) are the foundations of innovation. They're the basis for developing new ideas and creative solutions in response to problems in our world.

Companies must continually improve and develop their processes and products to remain relevant and successful. In turn, this opens up job opportunities that require creativity, confidence and an ability to collaborate and cooperate with others. STEM careers give huge job satisfaction and achieve higher-than-average pay.

» How can cadets develop STEM skills?

If you are part of Army Cadets you are already using STEM skills: team building, leadership, problem solving and thinking outside the box. Most jobs require skills like these.

In imaginative, project-based, multi-discipline challenges, cadets use STEM to solve problems modelled on real-world applications. For example, in Bedfordshire & Hertfordshire ACF a competition was run in which each company were asked to design and build the fastest non-motored remote-controlled vehicle to be raced at annual camp. It was hugely successful: all the cadets brought different skills to their teams and everyone learnt from each other. Given enough time, guidance and support, anything can be achieved.

To Inspire To Achieve

All photos: Peter Russell

Cadets learn how to move unexploded ordnance with the Royal Logistic Corps (RLC) during Exercise STEM Challenge at the Defence Academy at Shrivenham

Inspecting the Instant I2 drone during Exercise STEM Challenge at Westdown Camp

Introduction to equipment used by Explosive Ordnance Disposal (EOD) teams at Exercise STEM Challenge

» I'm interested in the military. How is STEM relevant?

STEM is used in all aspects of military life, from managing people and equipment to operating in the most difficult environments in the world.

The military needs the best people with the best ideas to ensure it remains effective and capable of achieving its objectives. Some of the most innovative ideas have come from our most junior soldiers; they have the ideas and solutions because they are the operators on the ground.

» Can I gain qualifications now?

Every year in Army Cadets there is a STEM challenge held in October half term which brings Corps from the British Army to showcase the applications of STEM within their unit. This provides cadets with an excellent opportunity to talk to soldiers about their experiences, and also to gain a STEM badge.

SMI Kate Dunscombe VR, Company Sergeant Major 3 Company, Bedfordshire & Hertfordshire ACF, is a Signal Engineer for London Underground and a Reservist with the Royal Engineers. She has led numerous Army Cadets STEM events.

⩗ Go further

Take your STEM skills to the next level

- Take up a STEM hobby
- Research STEM careers
- Visit STEM places of interest
- Take part in STEM competitions
- Visit STEM workplaces
- Get careers information from STEM Ambassadors
- Record your achievements to show future employers
- Research apprenticeships, colleges and universities

(www.stem.org.uk)

STEM CAMP 2020

2020's virtual STEM camp (Exercise STEM Challenge) may have looked a little different due to the pandemic, but it still featured a jam-packed mix of interactive activities, fascinating presentations and exciting challenges delivered by the Army's leading STEM experts. **1st (Northern Ireland) Bn C Coy STEM Ambassador Shirley Montgomery** reveals what went down.

Each year cadets are invited to a five-day camp delivered by specialist STEM experts. The pandemic put a stop to our face-to-face camp in 2020, but in true Army Cadets fashion we weren't deterred. From October 26–29, we took the camp online – and the results were fantastic.

Day 1

Ex STEM Challenge got off to a flying start on the first morning with the Army Air Corps (AAC) who kicked off with a presentation on Helicopters and Airfoil Technology. Cadets also learnt which AAC aircraft are best suited to different wartime and humanitarian applications.

The Royal Electrical and Mechanical Engineers (REME) gave an excellent demonstration on vehicle cooling systems. Cadets then participated in a virtual escape-room activity involving a vehicle breakdown.

After lunch, the Royal Artillery (RA) led a fascinating session looking at the physics, chemistry and geography behind locating (FIND) and destroying (STRIKE) the enemy using visual, audio and radar identification platforms.

In the evening, Army Cadets National Ambassador Craig Mathieson from The Polar Academy gave an inspirational and informative talk on how the Academy helps young people who struggle with self-esteem and anxiety to make positive transformations in their lives through exploration and adventure.

Day 2

The Royal Logistics Corps (RLC) gave cadets a comprehensive overview of STEM careers. Cadets were then able to take part in a virtual Explosive Ordinance Disposal (EOD) activity, solving clues in order to make safe a number of bombs.

The Royal Engineers (RE) also talked about the wide variety of STEM roles within the Corps and used QR codes to give cadets real-time access to online GEOtech mapping tools used to conduct terrain analysis and measure features such as area, distance and population density of user-defined areas.

Day 3

Cadets were joined by the Intelligence Corps and challenged to take part in Project TITAN. They were given mission details and multiple intelligence sources to establish and define Project TITAN's completion date.

The Army Medical Service demonstrated live simulations of a number of scenarios involving the decision-making process applied (and the consequences) when approaching and treating casualties, and also when using search dogs on patrols.

In the evening, cadets participated in a STEM careers webinar in which serving military personnel described how they use STEM in their day-to-day roles.

Day 4

The final day of Ex STEM Challenge saw cadets finishing on a high with some brain-busting codebreaking and logical analysis with the Royal Signals, as well as interactive forensic investigation activities with the Adjutants General Corp.

Every cadet who completed the camp was awarded the Army Cadets STEM Badge and the eTrust Industrial Cadets Award.

Feedback from the cadets on the camp was excellent.

Photo: Andy King

Cadet Cpl Lily Miller of Bedford Detachment attended the 2020 virtual STEM Camp:

'Thank you for helping me get onto this year's STEM camp. I really enjoyed it and it opened my eyes to the variety of STEM roles within the Army.

'I enjoyed it so much I gave a presentation on it yesterday at detachment – as well as on the iDEA award and CyberFirst (both of which I did over the summer) – so my cadet friends can know about it and apply in good time next year.'

Lily has used iDEA (she has achieved both Bronze and Silver Awards) and the STEM course as part of her DofE Silver Skills module training/learning, in addition to another online course with the Open University.

Lily's Detachment Commander SI Danny Ward said: *'Lily is keen and also very good at encouraging and supporting younger cadets at her detachment.'*

VIRTUAL training

With training taking place online for much of 2020-21, what has the experience been like for cadets and CFAVs? Read on to learn about the trials and the triumphs.

To Inspire To Achieve

» SSI Shaun Fudge

**Lytchett & Upton
Detachment, Dorset ACF**

'At the beginning of the first lockdown I could see everything would come crashing down unless we kept the cadets occupied and

held virtual recruitment evenings on Zoom with parents. They encouraged their children to join, and from that we ended up recruiting six new adult volunteers too.

'As parents are the ones who support the cadets, I keep in touch with them via parents' evenings, Messenger and email.'

'We didn't stop because we didn't want to go back to an empty detachment'

in touch,' says Shaun. *'So we held virtual training every Monday and Thursday from the first lockdown.*

'We didn't stop because we didn't want to lose any cadets and go back to an empty detachment. I also started a recruitment campaign using every possible media platform. We recruited 15 new cadets and I ended up having to transfer some of them to other detachments because there were too many.'

Shaun's main tactic was to target parents first: *'I used Facebook and posted on public groups, then*

Shaun knows training is important for the cadets' wellbeing and says: *'They rely on it. I told them at the beginning, "As long as you turn up, I'll turn up".*

'The virtual training went really well. I went through all of the theory training that could be done so that, when we resumed face-to-face training, my cadets would be confident in theory practices.'

Shaun has been promoted to Colour Sergeant and received a Commander South West's Coin for his recruitment drive and virtual training efforts.

'It was amazing to join and become part of something special during lockdown'

» PI Barrylee Warren

Barrosa Company, Hampshire and Isle of Wight ACF

Navigating the change from in-person to online training was challenging for CFAVs, but Barrylee says the encouragement of the Army Cadets organisation helped.

'I'm a qualified teacher and I like face-to-face teaching, so I found the virtual training tough at times, but everyone at the ACF was phenomenal,' he says.

» Lilia Jowett

Lytchett & Upton Detachment, Dorset ACF

Lilia, 13, was one of Shaun's new recruits and says: *'It was amazing to join and become part of something special during lockdown. It gave me something to do and helped improve my confidence.*

'It was easy to join virtually: I used a laptop for training but lots of people used their phones or tablets.'

In addition to learning a great deal, Lilia enjoyed the contact with others. She says: *'We covered a lot in our virtual training, including PT sessions, first-aid training, military knowledge and navigation, but we also had time to chat about what we'd been up to, and talk with our leaders.*

'I'm so glad I've joined – I love the feeling of being part of a team.'

'We gained new cadets during lockdown and also took on some new adult instructors'

'The organisation – including everyone at Barrosa Company – worked tirelessly. We were kept informed about what training was on each week and there was no shortage of information. They kept us in the loop and pumped a lot of time and effort into the virtual materials.

'We gained new cadets during lockdown and also took on some new adult instructors with a passion to pass their skills on to young cadets.'

'It made lockdown so much better because it was something to look forward to during the week'

» Jasmine Stroud

Lytchett & Upton Detachment, Dorset ACF

Jasmine, 15, joined the same Dorset detachment as Lilia during lockdown.

'I wanted to join because I had friends who were already cadets, who said it's like being part of another family.

'Joining virtually meant we raced through all the classroom lessons and tests, so that in face-to-face training we'll get to do the fun hands-on activities.

'I made new friends because of it. We messaged via social media and it's so nice now we can see each other in person.

'It made lockdown so much better because it was something to look forward to during the week.'

» Lieutenant and Detachment Commander Mhairi Jack

1 Platoon Royal Scots Borderers, Glasgow and Lanarkshire ACF

Going virtual enabled Mhairi to introduce new teaching methods to train young cadets.

'We tried to come up with new ideas of how we could work interactively,' she says. *'For instance, we asked cadets to practise activities with their parents and send us pictures and videos rather than doing it live because that can be nerve-racking for some.'*

'We created Lego maps and found it an easy way to explain contour lines'

One of the challenges of virtual sessions is the physical element of training, something Mhairi tried to adapt to: *'I knew senior cadets might have been missing out the most because their training is very practical.*

'We used everything from Lego to cardboard cutouts. Lego is a brilliant tool for navigation training; we created Lego maps and found it an easy way to explain contour lines.'

Army Cadets in
April 2021

Life-saving CPR

A man's life was saved when Sergeant Major Derek Ross of Castle Douglas Detachment was able to help a member of the public carry out CPR.

Derek was driving when he saw a man performing chest compressions on a casualty who had collapsed. He stopped and was able to help by taking over chest compressions and administering rescue breaths (using a CPR face-shield he had in the car) and four shocks via a defibrillator sourced from a local shop.

After a 28-minute delay, the ambulance arrived and the pair were able to hand over the casualty, who had regained a pulse and was breathing.

Photo: Sarah Potter

'Being a cadet makes me proud and happy'

» Diversity Month

The Army Cadets Inspire Twitter page – run by ACF's National Diversity and Inclusivity Adviser Colonel Darren Hughes – featured inspiring online videos created by cadets and CFAVs to promote and celebrate Diversity Month during April.

'Being a cadet makes me proud and happy and allows me to try new things. I like having fun and having friends in the Cadets,' said Lance Corporal Niquita Potter (pictured) from Devon ACF in a video shared on the channel. Niquita has Down's syndrome and was previously featured as BFBS Radio's Cadet of The Week due to her incredible fundraising achievements.

To mark Diversity Month and World Autism Day, Lance Corporal Gailey of 1st Battalion Northern Ireland ACF gave an insight into her personal experience of being autistic and a cadet. She said: *'I have been part of the Cadets for four years. Two years ago I was diagnosed with autism, but I've been able to have exactly the same experiences and participate in all the activities as other cadets. The ACF has been very accepting of who I am.'*

Photos: Kate Knight

» New air rifles and target screens arrive

CTC Frimley Park was delighted to officially receive the new Cadet Scorpion Air Rifles which were presented by Major General David Eastman MBE.

General Eastman tested the equipment (pictured) which is due to be available at all contingents and detachments by the end of 2021.

The air rifles were accompanied by new Cadet Air Rifle Indoor Target Screens, which have been developed using Nottinghamshire ACF's prototype.

General Eastman said: *'Shooting has been a staple of the cadet experience for many years and is considered one of the most exciting activities any young person will do in the Army Cadets.*

'It is the main activity that differentiates us from most other youth organisations. To be able to offer the latest top-of-the-range equipment to our cadets and CFAVs is fantastic and I hope they all enjoy it.'

'Shooting is considered one of the most exciting activities any young person will do in the Army Cadets'

FOOD

FOOD

Find out which foods adventurers eat
on their travels (spoiler: raw catfish
and Haribo feature), and learn a life skill
that keeps on giving: the art of baking.

FOODIE TIPS
from top adventurers

Ever been offered reindeer stew, tasted chicken feet or munched on raw seal? We asked some of our favourite adventurers for their top food tips, recipes and memorable foodie experiences from expeditions.

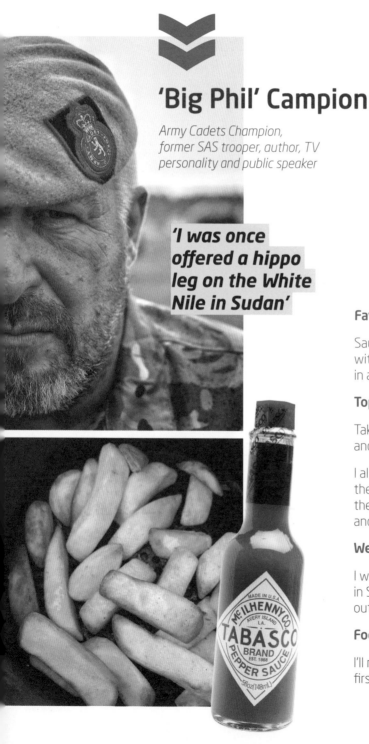

'Big Phil' Campion

Army Cadets Champion, former SAS trooper, author, TV personality and public speaker

'I was once offered a hippo leg on the White Nile in Sudan'

Favourite food for adventuring?

Sausage and beans, issued or homemade, with hot-dog sausages and baked beans in a sealed bag – shaken not stirred.

Top tips?

Take plenty of stuff you can eat hot or cold, and food you can eat on the hoof.

I also recommend three-in-one teabags (where the tea, milk and sugar come in one sachet). I use the pre-made ones, but you can mix them yourself and take a bag made up and ready to go.

Weirdest foodie experience on expedition?

I was once offered a hippo leg on the White Nile in Sudan. I declined on the grounds I had run out of Tabasco sauce – it didn't smell good.

Foodie memory?

I'll never forget making proper homemade chips on my first fresh ration day during my first trip to the jungle.

'On Everest we had barrels of high-energy bars that were, frankly, inedible'

Rebecca Stephens MBE

First British woman to climb Everest and the Seven Summits (the highest mountain on each continent), author, journalist and motivational speaker

Top foodie tips for adventurers?

Pack food you love: the tastiest and the most delicious. I say this because we had a nutritionist on Everest who supplied us with barrels of high-energy bars which were returned uneaten because they were, frankly, inedible.

Dos and don'ts?

Loss of appetite is a serious consideration at altitude, but isn't food to be enjoyed wherever we are? Maybe avoid squashy, melty foods (I'm thinking tomatoes or my favourite, chocolate) in a rucksack on a hot day. A bag of mixed nuts and raisins, or dates, are always a good (and delicious) standby.

FOODIE TIPS
from top adventurers

'Dairy Milk is a disaster in sub-zero temperatures!'

Roz Savage MBE

Speaker, author and ocean rower – Roz was the first woman to row solo across the Atlantic, Pacific and Indian Oceans

'I grew my own beansprouts on board'

Bear Grylls

Adventurer, writer and TV presenter

Best food for adventurers?

Honey and oat flapjacks are a winner for energy and morale on expeditions and exercises.

Pouches of almond or peanut butter are also easy, taste great and are packed with energy.

My go-to protein bars are by Grenade – they're delicious and healthy.

Foods to avoid?

Dairy Milk is a disaster in sub-zero temperatures!

What food do you eat during ocean adventures?

On my trip rowing the three oceans I had to take enough food on my boat to last up to five months. It had to be durable, calorie-dense and lightweight, but also healthy, nutritious and as environmentally friendly as I could manage. I also had to enjoy it.

Over the course of the journey, I got my diet down to a fine art: lots of nuts, dried fruit, porridge, rawfood crackers and snack bars. I had just one freeze-dried meal a day – they're quite heavily processed and I prefer to eat things closer to their natural state.

I also grew my own beansprouts on board. I mixed them with tahini, almonds and soy sauce to boost the calorie count.

Advice for aspiring adventurers?

Food is really important – emotionally, mentally and physically – so give it the attention it deserves. As with every other aspect of an expedition, failing to plan is planning to fail.

Jordan Wylie

Army Cadets National Ambassador, extreme adventurer, author and TV presenter

Favourite outdoors food?

There's nothing more rewarding than catching your own food, and fish makes a quick and easy meal if you're on an adventure. You can cook any type of fish in foil over a grill or fire. I'd suggest squeezing a little lemon over and sprinkling the fish with salt and pepper, garlic, rosemary, paprika or even Tabasco from your ration pack.

Tastiest food from your travels?

One particularly tasty dish was a camel burger in Mogadishu, Somalia.

And the strangest?

Chicken feet! I had them on board a Chinese vessel in the Indian Ocean.

Any food safety tips for aspiring adventurers?

Drink water from sealed containers (when in doubt, treat the water with a filtering system) and use safe water for rinsing food and brushing your teeth.

Boil unpasteurised milk and ensure food is cooked thoroughly before eating. Also avoid uncooked shellfish, undercooked eggs and meat, and food that's been exposed to insects.

'Chicken feet! I had them on board a Chinese vessel in the Indian Ocean'

FOODIE TIPS
from top adventurers

Photo: A360DEGREES

Craig Mathieson

Army Cadets National Ambassador, explorer, founder of The Polar Academy, Explorer-in-Residence with the Royal Scottish Geographical Society

Fave expedition food?

Wine gums are my ultimate pick-me-up. If I need to pull a sledge up a hill I think, *That's a six-wine-gum hill* which is guaranteed to get me up there. I mix wine gums with salami, dried fish and cheese for a combination of fat, protein and sugar.

What do you eat when exploring?

On polar expeditions, it has to be whatever I can find. In Greenland I fish for Arctic char, then pick local mushrooms, stuff them in the fish and fry it. For dessert I'll pick blueberries.

I go out with the Inuit a lot in the Arctic so I'll eat seal, whale or polar bear as that's what the locals survive on – it's very tasty. I always take garlic, salt and pepper to go with seal: that's a meal fit for a king.

The Inuit equivalent of Red Bull is a superfood called mattak, which is a layer of narwhal skin that you eat raw (you put it in the corner of your mouth and let it dissolve over hours). It's packed with vitamin c and, like Marmite, people love it or hate it.

'In Greenland I fish for Arctic char, pick local mushrooms, stuff them in the fish and fry it'

Local hunters love Greenland shark – it's their equivalent of wine gums – though I've never acquired a taste for it.

Once I had to clean my teeth for two days solid to get the taste of raw catfish fat out of my mouth. It's bright yellow and very nutritious when eaten raw – a thing most people only do once.

What food-related kit do you take?

In summer, virtually zero. Not even a water bottle, just a cup as I drink from the rivers. My top tip for food kit, though, is to always know where your spoon is! I always suggest keeping it in the right hand side of your jacket pocket. I've actually modified my mug to fit my spoon so they are always together.

Sally Orange

Army Cadets National Ambassador, endurance runner, adventurer and mental health champion

Photo: Kate Knight

Favourite food for adventuring?

I like the dehydrated expedition food made by Firepot. Last year I skied across a plateau in Norway and took them with me. They use compostable, eco-friendly packaging which is a bonus.

Best expedition snack?

Flapjack with raisins and pumpkin seeds. They're so easy to make at home before an expedition and are packed full of energy, flavour and texture.

'You can never go wrong with Haribo'

Peanut M&Ms are a good option for chocolate that won't melt. Add it to trail mix with lots of nuts for an energy-packed, flavourful snack. And you can never go wrong with Haribo.

Top foodie tips for adventuring?

Eat little and often. If you're adventuring at altitude, force yourself to eat – set an alarm because time goes by and you don't want to go for hours without eating.

Check in with your friends to make sure they are eating regularly too. Double up and make portions for two to share; working together as a team is just as important when it comes to food as in other areas.

Vivid food memories?

I did an expedition in the jungle and we had to hunt for our own food – we ate pig and chicken. I also ate reindeer stew in Norway.

Sometimes the most simple food tastes amazing on expedition. I remember thinking a Polo mint tasted like the best thing ever.

SPECIAL OFFER!

Exclusive to Army Cadets members

Staying healthy in the wild is key to a successful expedition. Firepot – praised by Army Cadets National Ambassador Sally Orange – provides an award-winning range of healthy, lightweight and nutritious dehydrated meals that are packed with nutrition. They are also recommended by the Duke of Edinburgh's Award as a key part of any kit list.

The meals are handmade in Dorset using fresh, local, natural ingredients and contain twice the amount of meat per meal as other well-known brands. There are vegan and gluten-free options available to order, as well as extra-large portions.

Stuff your rucksack with the likes of toasted banana porridge, barbecued pulled pork, spicy pork noodles and chicken keema curry. This is expedition food for every extreme and is ready in minutes when you're in need of a hot and satisfying meal – just add water.

The team at Firepot have offered a 15 per cent discount on its meals to all members of Army Cadets. Apply discount code **CADETS22** when you reach the checkout on the Firepot website. Code valid until 11.30pm on 31/12/22.

BAKING FOR BEGINNERS

Learning to bake is a life skill that's fun and relaxing, resulting in delicious treats to share with family and friends. Ready to hit up some easy recipes? Ready, steady, bake!

This recipe by Sarah Liveing (@ liveingbakes) is so quick and easy that even the most inexperienced baker is guaranteed success.

Peanut butter chocolate-chip cookies

› Ingredients

(makes about 15)

Unsalted, unroasted peanuts 50g

Unsalted butter 125g

Smooth peanut butter 125g

Golden caster sugar 100g

Soft, light brown sugar 100g

Egg 1, large and lightly beaten

Plain flour 200g

Salt ½ tsp

Bicarbonate of soda ½ tsp

Plain chocolate chips or chocolate cut into chunks 100g

› Method

1. Preheat the oven to 200°c/gas 6.

2. Roast the peanuts for 8–10 minutes on a baking tray. Leave to cool then roughly chop.

3. Melt the butter and peanut butter together in a medium saucepan over a low heat.

4. Allow the butters to cool then, using a wooden spoon, add the sugars and egg and mix thoroughly.

5. In a medium mixing bowl, mix the flour, salt and bicarbonate of soda.

6. Make a well in the dry ingredients, then add the wet ingredients and combine thoroughly.

7. Add the chocolate chips and roasted nuts, then cover and allow to chill in the fridge for up to an hour.

8. Remove the dough from the fridge and cut into pieces that weigh between 40–65g (40g will give you 7cm cookies and 65g will give you 8cm cookies). Roll the pieces into balls and place on a lined baking tray, leaving 2.5-3cm between each cookie.

9. Gently push the top of each one to flatten it slightly. Bake for 13-15 minutes. Allow to cool a little before placing the cookies on a wire rack to cool completely.

Why spend money on expedition snacks when you can bake your own and cram them full of nutritious nuts, seeds, berries and oats? **Kate Percy**, author of *Go Faster Food*, shares her winning recipe.

Ultimate energy bars

Slow-release energy is the name of the game when choosing snacks for expeditions, but that doesn't have to mean buying expensive sports snacks when they're easy to make at home.

The size and weight of the snack are also important: ideal expedition sustenance is calorie-dense for its size, so you don't have to carry more bulk than you absolutely need to. That's why these dense energy bars, packed full of nutritious ingredients, hit the spot.

'They're crammed with fruit, nuts and seeds,' says Kate. *'Sweetened condensed milk and peanut butter are used as a binder instead of butter and syrup, but those with a peanut allergy can use almond or cashew butter as an alternative.'*

And, fortunately, the bars won't be spoiled if they get squashed in a rucksack or, like chocolate, melt in warm weather.

> Ingredients

(makes 12 bars)

Condensed milk 397g can

Crunchy peanut butter 1 tbsp

Pumpkin or sunflower seeds (or mixture) 80g

Poppy seeds 20g

Mixed chopped dates, sultanas and cranberries 150g

Desiccated coconut (optional) 100g

Porridge oats (half regular, half jumbo) 240g

Beginners' baking tips

1. Follow the recipe Baking is science in action, so the relationship between the ingredients – especially the fat, flour, sugar and egg – really matters. Experienced chefs know if they keep these key ratios in place they can play with other ingredients and size up or size down a recipe. However, for beginner bakers following the recipe is the secret to success.

2. Hit the beat When a cake recipe calls for the fat and sugar to be beaten, that means beating it really hard so it turns a lighter shade and goes fluffy. The easiest way to do this is with a hand whisk or kitchen mixer, although it's possible to achieve exactly the same result with a wooden spoon.

3. Flour power When making a cake, after you've added the flour aim to stir or handle the mixture as little as possible to avoid working the gluten, as this will make the cake tough. The exact opposite is the case when making bread: kneading a bread mixture develops the gluten which gives the bread structure.

4. All in the timing Always set a timer as it's so easy to get distracted and let your baked goods burn. A good tip is to set the timer for a few minutes before the recipe states – just in case your oven is especially fierce. Another skill experienced bakers employ is to use their sense of smell. If baked goods smell cooked they often are cooked, so if your biscuits look golden, feel firm to the touch and smell delicious, trust your instinct and take them out of the oven, even if there are still a couple of minutes left on the timer.

〉 Method

1. Preheat the oven to 140°c/gas 1.

2. Grease and line an 18cm x 25cm baking tray.

3. Pour the condensed milk into a saucepan and gently warm.

4. Stir in the peanut butter, then add the rest of the ingredients and mix well.

5. Spoon the mix onto the baking tray and gently flatten down with the back of the spoon, pushing the mix so it reaches the edges.

6. Bake in the oven for 50–60 minutes until golden brown.

7. Allow the tray to cool a little then mark out squares using a sharp knife. Leave to cool further before gently lifting the squares out to cool completely on a wire rack. The bars will keep in an airtight container for days.

With this easy-to-make chocolate sponge recipe up your sleeve you'll have birthdays and celebrations covered – though it's just as good on a wet Sunday afternoon.

Chocolate cake for beginner bakers

› Ingredients

For the cake:

Butter or margarine 285g (plus some for the tin)

Caster sugar 285g

Eggs 5

Self-raising flour 235g (plus some for the tin)

Cocoa powder 40g

Baking powder 1 tsp

For the chocolate icing:

Butter 125g, soft (at room temp)

Icing sugar 140g

Cocoa powder 15g

Water 5g, cold

Milk 1 dessert spoon

How to prepare a cake tin

In order to stop a cake from sticking to the side of the tin during cooking, it's essential to prepare the tin before putting the cake mixture in it. Do this is by smearing a light coating of butter or margarine over the entire inside of the tin, taking care not to miss any areas. Then add in a couple of dessert spoons of flour and tilt the tin, tapping as you go, until flour has stuck to the entire inside of the tin. Pour any excess flour away.

❯ Method

1. Preheat the oven to 180°c /gas 4.

2. Prepare (see notes above) an approximately 20cm x 20cm cake tin (any shape).

3. Put the butter or margarine and the caster sugar in a mixing bowl. If you have one, use the mixing bowl of a kitchen mixer such as a Kenwood Chef or KitchenAid. If not, put the fat and sugar in the largest bowl you have. Beat the two ingredients – using the machine, a hand whisk or a wooden spoon – until it turns pale.

4. Lightly beat the eggs in a small bowl and pour into the fat and sugar mixture. Stir well to combine.

5. Pour the flour, cocoa and baking powder into a separate bowl and combine. Pour these dry ingredients into the wet mixture and gently stir together until just combined.

6. Very gently, pour the cake mixture into the prepared tin and bake for 35–40 minutes until the cake is firm to the touch on top and slightly shrinks from the sides of the tin. To check the cake is cooked all the way through, pierce it through the centre with a metal skewer (or a sharp knife). If it comes out clean, the cake is cooked. If there is some wet mixture on the skewer, cook for five more minutes, then test again.

7. When the cake is cooked, let it cool then decorate it using melted chocolate (which will set solid when cold) or with chocolate butter icing. To make this, beat the ingredients (listed left) and spread over the top of the cake.

Beginners' baking tips (continued)

5. Egg 'em on It's good to be mindful of the kind of eggs you use and, if possible, do your bit for animal welfare by buying free-range eggs. You'll know an egg is fresh when you crack it open, as the yolk and white of a fresh egg will be firm and sit up proudly. That's ideal for poached or fried eggs, but a slightly older egg with a flatter yolk and more runny white is perfectly fine to use in baking.

6. Room temperature When baking cakes or bread, aim to get the ingredients out of the fridge an hour before you start so they can get to room temperature. However, if you're making pastry – or even a crumble topping – cold fat is essential to help you rub it into the flour.

7. Rise to the top Bicarb and baking soda are not the same thing, even though they're both raising agents (which help make cakes light) and come in similar packages. Bicarb (or bicarbonate of soda) is a pure raising agent that needs moisture and acid to make it work, while baking powder is a mix of bicarb and cream of tartar (which provides the acid to activate the bicarb). If you don't have any baking powder use bicarb instead, but halve the amount and add something acidic such as a spoonful of lemon juice, buttermilk or even cocoa to activate it.

Army Cadets in
May 2021

» CFAV gives vital first aid in roadside incident

SI Ryan Doran of D Company's Spen Valley Detachment was driving to work when he was flagged down in the town of Hipperholme by a passerby who told him a boy had been hit by a car.

As a first-aid-trained CFAV, Ryan immediately went to assist the 14-year-old.

'I could see a gentleman trying to lift him up from where he was lying and that's when I decided to take over the situation'

'He was rolling about and screaming about his neck,' said Ryan. 'I could see a gentleman trying to lift him up from where he was lying and that's when I decided to take over the situation.

'While carrying out the First Aid Primary Survey, I quickly established that we needed to keep him still because of the neck pain. He was also complaining of stomach and head pain.

'The teenager's backpack straps were very tight around his shoulders, so his dad and uncle cut them to relieve the pressure, but I made sure they did not then move the bag.

'I realised I had to keep his head and neck still, and I asked his mother to keep his legs still as well.

'The lad had a big bump on the side of the head, which was a concern. I also suspected one of his shoulders was dislocated or broken.'

Throughout the ordeal, SI Doran continued to talk to the teenager, making sure he was as comfortable as possible, as well as reassuring family members.

When the ambulance arrived, the crew asked SI Doran to continue keeping the teenager's head and neck still while they carried out observations. The police also attended and the teenager was taken to hospital.

Later that day, SI Doran was able to visit the teenager's home to get an update on his condition, learning that he had sustained a broken shoulder (which required surgery), a broken leg, and cuts and bruising to his face and arms.

Ryan was nominated for a national ACFA Praiseworthy First Aid Award for his prompt and effective actions.

» Pennine power

Newquay Detachment Commander Angela Mckendrick from Cornwall completed a charity trek along the Pennine Way (268 miles from the Peak District to the Scottish borders) with six veterans to raise awareness and funds for post-traumatic stress disorder (PTSD).

Although Angela isn't a veteran, she took part in the challenge to support friends and family who have sought help from PTSD organisations.

Angela said: *'The first time I walked up a hill I was puffing and by the time I got to the top I was gasping for breath. I wondered what I'd got myself into.'*

Being part of a team helped her through setbacks and the physical and emotional challenge of the gruelling trek. *'Sometimes it just takes the right mindset and the right people to pave the way,'* she added.

The team's 16-day walk raised £16,000 and they've been awarded the Colonel of the Regiment's Commendation.

» Award for cadet

Cadet Sgt Rosie Nelson from A Company's Malton Detachment received an award from the Fellmongers Company in recognition of her outstanding volunteer work. She was praised for her proactive efforts to improve the physical and mental health of members of her community during the Covid-19 pandemic. Her actions included creating face masks for family, friends and neighbours.

CYCLE SUCCESS

Cadets were challenged to compete in a virtual cycle challenge by cycling 70 miles (representing the distance around the Isle of Wight) throughout May, taking photos and videos along the way. The aim was to introduce cycling into Army Cadet Sports. All the cadets and CFAVs who took part did a brilliant job of stepping up to the challenge, but staff at CTC Frimley Park took it one step further, completing an impressive 70 miles in a single day.

Cambridgeshire ACF cadets Isaac Lawrence and Aimee Corby, and SI Lloyd Lester, all of Huntingdon Detachment, and Cadet Aaron Joyce of St Ives Detachment

Bear with ...

Through the Every Cadet project, cadets and CFAVs (with help from a cuddly accomplice) have done an ace job of raising the profile of the Duke of Edinburgh's Awards this year.

The official launch of an exciting campaign to encourage all Army Cadets to take part in the Duke of Edinburgh's Award (DofE) kicked off on 1 March via a live Facebook event.

National DofE Award Advisor Major Dan Tebay said: *'The aim of the Every Cadet project is that every cadet gains the DofE Award.'*

The project centred around four clear aims: to ensure every cadet is offered, enrolled on, supported through, and enabled to complete the DofE in the Army Cadets.

To help spread the word, a toolkit was issued, and cuddly bears – to be shared using the hashtag #EveryCadetBear – were sent to each county to join cadets on their DofE activities.

The project was a huge hit, with the hashtag trending and images shared far and wide. Read on for a taste of what the Every Cadet bear got up to.

Cadet Lance Corporal Toby Spear of West Buckland School CCF

The bear made it to the TV studio of Army Cadets National Honorary Colonel Lorraine Kelly

'The project was a huge hit, with the hashtag trending far and wide'

Army Cadets DofE
@ACFADofE

Yesterday #EveryCadetBear did his first kayak expedition (45km!) along the River Dart and out into the sea. His aim was to spot wildlife; he saw grey seals, harbour porpoises and a peregrine falcon! What a lucky bear, thanks to the amazing @sally0range 🚣
@ACFColCadets

8:00 PM · Jul 22, 2021 · Twitter for iPhone

Army Cadets National Ambassador Sally Orange let the bear hitch a ride on her cycling adventure

Lance Corporal Oli Messenger of St Edward's School Cheltenham CCF

Cadet David Gillvary of Cumbernauld Detachment

Lance Corporal Tang and Lance Corporal Buckley of Haberdashers' CCF caving at the Cadet Centre for Adventurous Training

#EveryCadetBear's Twitter takeover

Berkshire ACF DofE
@BerksACF_DofE

Day one of #berkshireacf annual camp, and I'm making sure the DofE message gets spread far and wide #acf #armycadets #dofe @ACFADofE

2:29 PM · Jul 24, 2021 · Twitter for iPhone

2nd (NI) Battalion ACF
@2NIACF

The "Every Cadet" bear has arrived in Northern Ireland today to help kickstart DofE activity over the coming months. Watch out for what our #EveryCadetBear gets up to and what is happening to help you progress with your DofE.

#DofE #ACFADofE #ArmyCadetsUK @PadreBn @AcfComber

You and 9 others

Cadet Hettie Dixon of Godolphin School CCF

» Every Cadet competition

As a part of the Every Cadet project there was also a photo competition and a challenge for cadets to create recruitment materials for DofE in the Army Cadets.

Suffolk ACF cadets on expedition

» DofE expeditions return!

It was wonderful for units to kickstart expeditions again and see cadets making the most of the new expedition syllabus, which perfectly aligns with DofE expedition protocols.

Temporary changes were made to enable expeditions to be Covid-compliant, but that didn't stop cadets and CFAVs completing their awards and gaining achievements.

OC4Coy_CoLNESACF
@garrytooey

Is there any better picture then to see @ACFADofE @ACF_NELondon Bronze training expeds going ahead! Absolutely love it - thanks to my 4 Coy team today #everycadet #DofE #ACF

9:32 PM · Jun 5, 2021 · Twitter for Android

» Spectacular DofE results

Despite lockdown, cadets and CFAVs achieved an incredible

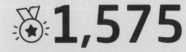 **1,575**

DofE Awards and Certificates of Achievement in 2020/2021.

Huge congratulations to all those who took part.

Army Cadets in
June 2021

Photo: Doug Stuart

Cpl Samantha Bowler-Legate with some of the cans, along with Major Lesley Deacon (left) and SSI Dave Moller

'It was great to see her continuing to put into practice the values she has learned'

›› Can-do cadet

Cdt Corporal Samantha Bowler-Legate was featured in her local paper the *Ely Standard* after she collected over 1,500 cans to raise funds for Helipads for Hospitals.

Samantha, from Cambridgeshire ACF, Waterbeach Detachment, set herself the challenge of collecting as many aluminium cans as possible in order to sell them for their scrap value. Her aim was to raise money for new landing areas at hospitals for emergency helicopters, as well as to improve helicopter access to and from the sites.

Samantha spent three months collecting the aluminium cans through social media appeals, her school and via a family member's workplace. Newmarket Racecourse even promised to pass on thousands of cans in the future to support the cause.

Samantha said: *'I'm really pleased with how many cans we collected – it was a lot more than I expected.*

'We had to crush the cans, and I got very competitive with my stepdad to see who could squash them the quickest!'

Samantha's mum Lesley and stepdad SSI Dave Moller are both private ambulance drivers and this inspired her to support medical causes.

She was introduced to volunteering through the Duke of Edinburgh Bronze Award, for which she helped organise a regular fundraising raffle for Cambs ACF and Defibrillators For All.

Following that experience, she started raising funds for Helipads for Hospitals, another cause supported by Cambs ACF.

Major Lesley Deacon, Deputy Commandant of Cambs ACF, said: *'We encourage our cadets to play an active part in their community and to put others before themselves.*

'Having learned these values in the ACF, and been encouraged to volunteer by participating in the Duke of Edinburgh's Award, it was great to see Cpl Bowler-Legate continuing to put into practice the values she has learned in order to help others.'

Well done Captain Kerry Barker!

Captain Kerry Barker transformed her lifestyle and increased her daily exercise during the national lockdowns, leading to a six-and-a-half-stone weight loss.

With her new dog by her side, the Assistant County Training Officer of Dorset ACF and Regional Manager at CVQO walked 10km each day and, once a month, increased that to 20-25km.

She said: *'Lockdown certainly made me re-evaluate my health, fitness and wellbeing for the better.'*

THIS GIRL CAN

❯❯ SHORTLIST CELEBRATIONS

Army Cadet Magazine was shortlisted in the CIPR Excellence Awards 2021 and Davos Communications Awards.

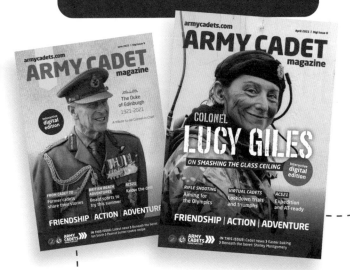

NEWS IN BRIEF

Photo: Pete Dodds

❯ Channel 4 show **SAS, Who Dares Wins** saw former cadet Justine Pellew-Harvey, from Falmouth Detachment, Cornwall, overcome gruelling mental and physical challenges to reach the final which aired in June. She said: *'My time in the ACF definitely helped me. When it came to time management, leadership tasks, respecting higher ranking staff, and navigation tasks, four years in the cadets came in handy!'*

❯ **13 Company South West London ACF** ran an appeal for food that could be used to create hampers for patients discharged from King's College Hospital – to tide them over until they were able to go out and buy food. Cadets helped the hospital's volunteer service distribute the hampers, too.

❯ **Suffolk Army Cadets** were celebrated in the *East Anglian Daily Times* for raising over £10,000 for NHS Charities Together, Suffolk Community Foundation and St John Ambulance.

The cadets, who smashed their initial target of £3,000, took part in a series of challenges, inspired by VE and VJ Days. Lt Col Rob Simpkin, Deputy Commandant of Suffolk ACF said: *'The benefits not only included the sums raised and physical ones from the activities, but also the mental-health gains of having a goal, staying focused and being able to help make a difference during Covid.'*

A REMARKABLE
CAREER

In the summer of 2021 **Lieutenant General Sir Tyrone Urch KBE** retired from the Army after 38 years' service. He shares the personal beliefs and mindset which shaped his astonishing military career.

Photo: LCpl Chris Bitten

Leaving in style: HQ Home Command and Standing Joint Command (UK) give General Sir Tyrone Urch KBE an emotional send-off

When did your interest in Army life begin?

My father was in the Army so we were an Army family 'following the flag'. Perhaps that's an old-fashioned view – I hope not. Anyway, I knew from a young age I wanted the same outdoor life, travel and comradeship.

I joined the CCF at school when I was 13 years old and it was very much the start of my military career. Although I didn't do brilliantly well, I do remember being promoted to the rank of cadet corporal, learning from my instructors and loving everything the CCF stood for.

How did your cadet experience prove useful in later life?

I learnt a lot about life and myself. I especially remember the adult volunteers who helped me so much. More than anything, being a cadet started to equip me with a confidence that's carried me through many difficult situations, both personally and professionally.

What would you tell your teenage self?

Don't doubt yourself. Have a go – be more pirate.

Who has inspired you?

Sir Ernest Shackleton, the greatest strategist and small-team leader rolled into one, ever (in my humble opinion).

What's helped you through challenging times?

The training in the Armed Forces is some of the best in the world, but you don't learn much by training easy. I got through by knowing I was never alone and that I always had my family or a buddy nearby.

As Commander Home Command, you had responsibility for recruiting. What kind of messages resonate with young people?

We recognise that a lot of our young recruits are interested in technology, video games and social media, and we have roles that fit all those interests. Cadets Branch HQ engages with young people in a language they understand and can relate to.

Our latest messaging also talks about a new sense of belonging, building confidence that lasts a lifetime, and the merit of being allowed to fail, learn and then win.

What was it like being Standing Joint Commander in the fight against Covid-19?

It was summarised best last year when I asked for feedback about how we were supporting the NHS. I was told our men and women brought:

- Discipline, no matter what the situation

- Tempo, at a time of crisis

- Resilience 24/7

- An ability to think outside the box

- A sense of humour

How does it feel to be leaving the Army?

I won't lie, after a 38-year career in uniform it is a little daunting, but I'm also incredibly excited. Without doubt, I will miss the people the most – be it regular, reserve, civil service, contractors or cadets. I often say, 'People *are* the Army, not *in* the Army'.

What does your next chapter look like?

Although I'm leaving the Army, this is not retirement for me. I really look forward to using what I've learnt to help other people manage complex projects and be better leaders. I also fancy doing a bit of teaching.

In my spare hours, I look forward to spending more time on my tractor and with the animals on our new family smallholding.

'Have a go – be more pirate'

At his leaving celebration at Montgomery House on 7 June , 2021

Photo: Lcpl Chris Butler

CAREER HIGHLIGHTS

In a distinguished career spanning almost four decades, Lieutenant General Urch has experienced a number of highlights. Recent ones include:

- Helping the Army achieve 100 per cent of its private soldier recruitment target during the last two years.

- Commanding thousands of Royal Navy, British Army and Royal Air Force personnel in support of the UK's fight against Covid-19, a task for which he was knighted in the 2021 New Year's Honours List.

- Coordinating the funeral of His Royal Highness The Duke of Edinburgh.

- Being Army Race Champion and giving ethnic minorities a voice at the Army Board table.

- Being selected by HM The Queen to be her Chief Royal Engineer.

- Winning his Service Squash Colours representing the British Army v Royal Navy (lost 3-1).

» Urch's reflections on life

I have a list of principles, which I call 'Urch's reflections on life', some of which are very relevant to cadets:

- Family first

- Pursue excellence

- Do the right thing on a bad day when no one is watching

- Leave it all on court

- Ask questions and be a good listener

- Prioritise ruthlessly

- Maintain a sense of humour

- Never lose your temper

- Make friends before you need them

- Look after yourself, your family and your friends

- Always ask: 'How can I best help you?'

A message for cadets

There is so much to look forward to now Covid-19 restrictions are finally easing.

Everyone at Cadets Branch HQ is working tirelessly to deliver the best possible cadet experience and I know cadets and adult volunteers are looking forward to getting back out and doing what we all love.

Thank you so much for sticking with it – you are all amazing individuals. Enjoy the journey.

Photo: LCpl Chris Butler

Photo: Major (ACF) John V Baxendale

'I've been given a lot of opportunities, so I'm looking forward to supporting other cadets as RSM'

» Highest-ranked Army Cadet in North Wales

Ethan Thompson was appointed to the senior rank of Cadet Regimental Sergeant Major (RSM) by Wrexham MP Sarah Atherton during summer camp.

The 17-year-old now leads and gives guidance to over 400 young people in Clwyd and Gwynedd ACF.

Sarah (pictured), who is a member of the Armed Forces Parliamentary Scheme and the Defence Select Committee, said: *'I was delighted to be able to make this presentation to this talented young man.'*

Ethan, from Rossett Detachment, has been a cadet for five years during which he has completed five summer camps and progressed to Master Cadet.

'I was very pleased to receive this promotion. It's something I've been working towards for some time but I never thought I'd progress this far,' he said.

'I've managed to do so much with the Cadets since joining. I've made some great friends and been given a lot of opportunities, so I'm looking forward to supporting other cadets as RSM.'

Detachment Commander Chalky White said: *'Ethan has always shown loyalty and commitment to both his company and detachment. He is a well-presented cadet on all occasions, showing a maturity we wish all cadets would grow into. This appointment is a just reward for his hard work and commitment.'*

Company Commander Andrea Burton added: *'Ethan has been an exemplary cadet and worked tirelessly during his time in Cadets. He's thoroughly deserving of this promotion.'*

Ethan has also been appointed a Lord-Lieutenants Cadet for 2021. This means he can be called upon to accompany Her Majesty's Lord-Lieutenant for Clwyd, Mr Henry Fetherstonhaugh Esq, at official engagements, including playing an active role in ceremonial events such as royal visits and Remembrance services held in Clwyd.

Photo: 2Lt Amanda Roxborough 1(NI) Bn ACF

» Anna-Grace gets The Diana Award

Cadet Anna-Grace Donnelly, 15, from Cullybackey Detachment, was honoured with The Diana Award at a ceremony which also marked the late Princess of Wales' 60th birthday.

The Award, established in memory of Diana, Princess of Wales, has the support of both her sons, The Duke of Cambridge and The Duke of Sussex, and is said to be 'the highest accolade a young person can achieve for social action or humanitarian efforts'. It's a legacy to Diana's belief that young people have the power to change the world.

Anna-Grace played a vital role in the distribution of food and essential supplies to the elderly and those at risk during the Covid-19 pandemic. She also encouraged other cadets to get involved, helping foster community spirit between groups of young people in her local area.

With the Cullybackey Community Partnership she maintained local flower displays and, along with Ballymena cadets from the Air and Sea Cadets, assisted in numerous village litter picks. She also helped homeschool her younger sibling during lockdowns.

Throughout the pandemic, Anna-Grace took part in virtual events such as Salute to Captain Tom, a VE Day Tea Party, the 1st (NI) Battalion ACF One-Mile Virtual Race, and a Battalion Video Sports Tribute to NHS staff. She also organised cadets in her detachment to place poppy crosses on the war graves of those killed in the two world wars, in conjunction with a project put forward by the Battalion's RSMI.

Anna-Grace has also been working towards her Gold Duke of Edinburgh's Award and the John Muir Environmental Award through Army Cadets.

Lord Lt and Honorary Col of the Cadets David McCorkell said of Anna-Grace: *'Since joining the Cadets in March 2019, she has devoted a great deal of her own time to helping others, as well as contributing to the environment and image of her local area. She has achieved much since joining and clearly lives up to our values and standards.'*

» Royal honour

Army Cadet Harry McDonough, along with Sea Cadet Alfie Allen and Air Cadet Sara Silva (pictured), had the honour of accompanying HRH Prince Charles, the Prince of Wales, as he toured the Great Yorkshire Show.

TRAINING

With the new ACS21 syllabus being launched, a lot of new training material has been developed to hone cadets' skills in areas from fieldcraft to drill. Read on to get clued up on what'll be going down.

Photo: Lieutenant Simon Crossley

Ready for ADVENTURE?

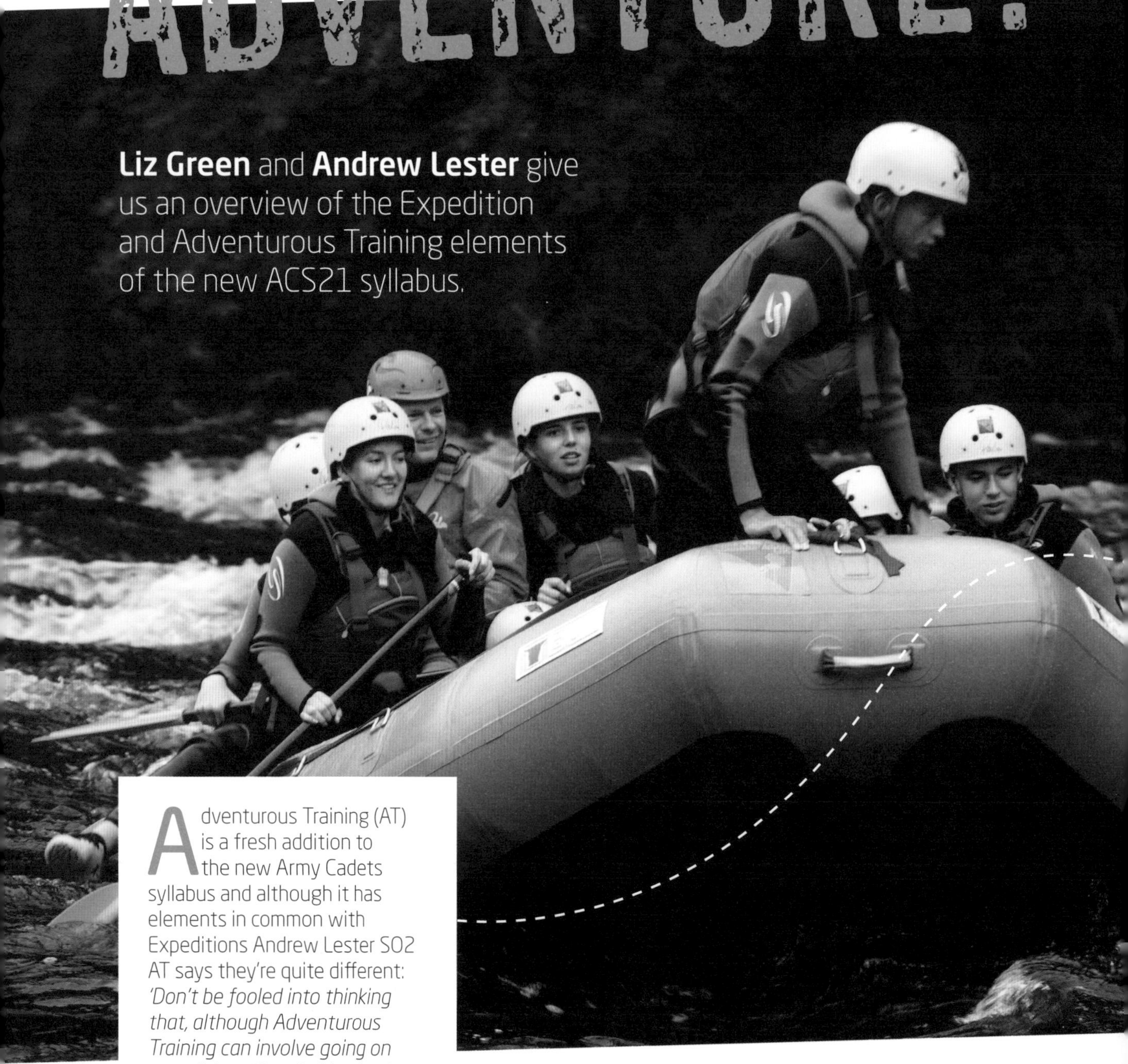

Liz Green and **Andrew Lester** give us an overview of the Expedition and Adventurous Training elements of the new ACS21 syllabus.

Adventurous Training (AT) is a fresh addition to the new Army Cadets syllabus and although it has elements in common with Expeditions Andrew Lester SO2 AT says they're quite different: *'Don't be fooled into thinking that, although Adventurous Training can involve going on expeditions like climbing in the Alps, that the two syllabuses are interchangeable.*

'AT will be a fantastic new addition to the training syllabus and is one of the main reasons young people join Army Cadets. It's fun, challenging and provides a well-established and recognised platform for personal development. It also has the added benefit of providing opportunities to travel.'

'Activities develop physical and mental robustness by exposing cadets and CFAVs to controlled risk'

Both AT and Expeditions are governed by the new AT and Expeds Manual, which has been written collaboratively. They're also both represented by Army Cadets National Ambassador Jordan Wylie, who says:

'Expeditions are one of the greatest learning environments available to young people. From planning and preparation through to the action-packed delivery phase, they take cadets on a journey which sees them push through perceived boundaries, both physically and mentally.'

Liz Green, SO2 DofE, who led the production of the Expedition Syllabus says:

'As well as providing lots of great new material and resources to support instructors, it fully aligns with DofE expeditions, meaning cadets can have "two for the price of one".

'We want cadets to have fun and challenging expedition experiences, learn more about themselves through being self-sufficient, and develop teamwork skills and self-reliance.

'They'll have an opportunity to use some of the skills they've learnt in other syllabus areas – such as first aid, leadership and navigation – and

apply these in practical situations. Expeditions in the Army Cadets should bring together many different strands of learning, and enable our young people to enjoy the outdoors, learn about themselves, and progress in both the syllabus and DofE.'

The benefits to cadets from both areas of training are significant. Andrew says: 'AT can be challenging and arduous at times, requiring courage, determination and self-discipline to succeed. The activities also develop physical and mental robustness by exposing cadets and CFAVs to controlled risk, enabling them to develop risk-management strategies. This helps create independent and responsible people.'

What's in the Army Cadets Expeditions and Adventurous Training manual?

- Policy
- Authorisation and assurance
- Activity planning
- Training on private land
- Clothing and equipment
- DofE and ACS21 expeditions
- Leading groups in normal country
- Activity specific guidance

KIT 101

With real-life expeditions back on the agenda, it's time to make sure you've got your kit know-how sorted.

Footwear

- Break in your boots early. Wear them as often as you can in different types of weather and terrain, and while carrying kit.

- Socks should ideally be chosen and bought before you buy your boots. They should have padding on the bridge, toes and heel to prevent rubbing. Liner socks can also be a good idea.

- When purchasing boots, try them on with the socks you plan to wear on expedition.

- There are many different ways to lace boots. Try various lacing styles and walk around in them to find the best one for you.

- Boots must have ankle support to protect you while you're carrying a heavy rucksack. They also need a deep tread for grip.

- When deciding how much to spend on new boots, consider how often you'll use them.

- Treat your boots properly before use to ensure they look after you on your venture. Clean boots well and let them dry naturally as soon as possible after wearing.

- Store boots in a dry, well-aired space. Don't store them wet as it can cause mould and rot.

Clothing

» Wear multiple layers of clothing

This will provide better insulation and even regulation of body temperature. Employing multiple layers is particularly important when you're likely to encounter changeable and unpredictable weather.

» Wear long-sleeved tops and lightweight trousers

This is preferable to T-shirts and shorts as they protect the skin.

» Avoid jeans, tracksuit bottoms and hoodies

They become heavy and can rub when wet.

Sleeping bag

A suitable sleeping bag and sleeping mat will greatly improve sleep quality. Sleeping bags generally come in season ratings:

- 1–2 season = summer
- 3 season = spring/autumn
- 4 season = winter

Choose a sleeping bag designed to be used at the lowest expected night-time temperature, as you can undo the zip if you're too warm.

TIP

Don't store sleeping bags in their stuffsacks as it damages their filling. Store hanging up or in a bin bag.

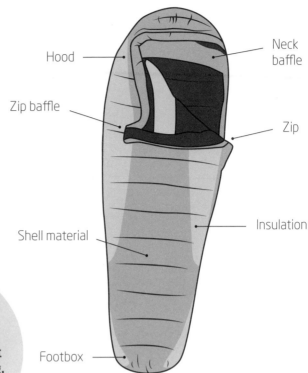

Hood · Neck baffle · Zip baffle · Zip · Shell material · Insulation · Footbox

⌃ A well-designed sleeping bag will have most of the features of the image above. A good hood, neck and zip baffle will improve insulating capability. Check the bag is of a suitable length – too short is uncomfortable while too long means carrying unnecessary weight.

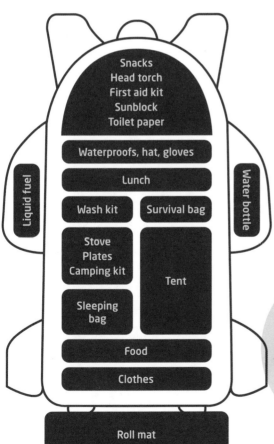

Snacks / Head torch / First aid kit / Sunblock / Toilet paper / Waterproofs, hat, gloves / Lunch / Wash kit / Survival bag / Stove Plates Camping kit / Tent / Sleeping bag / Food / Clothes / Roll mat / Liquid fuel / Water bottle

« Know how to pack your rucksack for effective and comfortable load carrying and appropriate access to equipment. Here's where everything goes.

TIP

When on expedition, you shouldn't carry kit that weighs more than 25 per cent of your body weight.

Rucksack

Key things to look for when choosing a rucksack:

- Strong and substantial waist belt.
- Wide and padded shoulder straps with an adjustable sternum buckle.
- A good number of pockets in suitable locations so you can separate kit when packing.
- An adjustable back system.

Thrill of the DRILL

Drill & Turnout is a key component of Army Cadet training, but do you know why? We talk to **Regimental Sergeant Major Jack Owen WO1** of CTC Frimley Park who reveals some surprising facts.

'After cadets have got to grips with the basics, they move on to drill with a rifle'

Photo: Lt Louise Wellman

» What is drill?

Drill is the term used to describe a formal parade where cadets are able to move quickly in formation from one place to another. This may sound easy, but when there is more than one person marching, turning and saluting at the same time it can be very difficult to master.

Cadets learn how to form into a squad, then progress to turning and saluting at a halt. Once they have mastered these moves separately, they are put together: marching, moving, turning and saluting on the march.

There are various levels of drill. After cadets have got to grips with the basics, they move on to drill with a rifle. After learning the drill routine they will then be taught the skills needed to teach others, including key command words and the art of timing.

» Why do cadets do it?

Drill helps cadets gain a better understanding of how they fit in and operate within a group, by learning how to march and being part of a team. It's an excellent way of encouraging vital skills like self-discipline and for developing a sense of pride.

» The new training manual covers both drill and turnout

Turnout is the term used to describe how to wear uniform and personal equipment correctly. Appearance is an important part of being a cadet and it is an individual's responsibility to always look smart and tidy when in Army Cadets uniform. Cadets learn about each part of their uniform and how to take care of it, ensuring smartness at all times.

» How relevant is drill in the 21st century?

Drill has evolved over a long period of time and is accepted as the foundation of military discipline. The main purpose of formal parade ground drill is to enable bodies of cadets to be moved easily and quickly from point to point in an orderly manner. In doing so, it has particular value for cadets in making them alert and teaching them to hold themselves properly.

» A surprising history

'The history of drill goes right back to the beginning of the Army Cadets,' says Regimental Sergeant Major Jack Owen WO1, 'as far back as 1859 when the threat of invasion from the French resulted in volunteer units being formed to repel a possible assault.

'Following this, the Cadets was formed when several volunteer units and schools started up their own Cadet Companies. One of these was the Queen's Westminsters, who placed their 35 cadets at the head of the formation when they marched past Queen Victoria in 1860.

'Miss Octavia Hill also formed a Southwark Cadet Company to introduce boys from slum areas to the virtues of cleanliness, teamwork and self-reliance. If we look at the discipline and confidence you can gain through working as part of a team on the drill square, you can see how the cadets of the past shared the same values as us.'

» Ceremonies and events

Drill delivers once-in-a-lifetime opportunities for young people to take part in historic ceremonies and events.

'Prince Philip's funeral was an excellent example of why drill is still relevant today,' says Jack. *'Sadly, due to Covid-19 restrictions, the planned inclusion of cadets from the Royal Navy, Army and Air Force was not possible, yet the ability of Army Cadets to take part in such parades is hugely significant.'*

'You can see how the cadets of the past shared the same values as us'

» The power of teamwork

In addition to its role in events, drill develops important skills that can influence many areas of cadets' lives.

'I still remember my first days in training at Guards Company in Pirbright,' says Jack. *'Drill formed a large part of my days which were spent preparing my kit and equipment, making sure I was as smart as could be, and helping others with their kit, as well as working as a team on the drill square.*

'For some, taking part in drill may be the first time they have been part of a team. You rely on the performance of others, manage how you work together towards a common goal, learn how to operate and fit in with a team, grow in confidence, and enjoy the sense of belonging that being part of a team creates.'

» Know your drill terms

Alignment A straight line on which a body of cadets/CFAVs is formed or is to form.

Covering Placing oneself directly behind another body.

Depth The space occupied by a body of cadets/CFAVs from front to rear.

Distance The space between cadets/CFAVs or bodies from front to rear.

Dressing Aligning oneself with and covering others within a body of cadets/CFAVs.

File a) Two or three cadets/CFAVs in different ranks who are covering each other. **b)** A body of cadets/CFAVs in two ranks facing a flank.

Single file Cadets/CFAVs one behind another on a frontage of one at normal marching distance.

Blank file A file in which there is no centre and rear body, or no centre body, due to the inequality of numbers within a body of cadets/CFAVs. This file is the second from the left in three ranks and the third from the left in two ranks.

Flank Either side of a body of cadets/CFAVs – as opposed to its front or rear.

Directing flank The flank by which a body of cadets/CFAVs takes its dressing.

Frontage The extent of ground covered laterally by a body of cadets/CFAVs, measured from flank to flank.

Interval The lateral space measured between cadets/CFAVs on the same alignment.

Line Cadets/CFAVs formed on the same alignment.

Markers Cadets/CFAVs employed to mark points on which a movement is to be directed, or by which a formation or alignment is to be regulated.

Order (close or open) The distance between ranks in line which is either 750mm (30 inches) or 1500mm (60 inches), depending on circumstances.

Rank A line of cadets/CFAVs side by side.

Supernumerary rank The extra rank, fourth rank in three ranks, or third in two ranks, formed by the senior NCOs.

NEW!

DRILL & TURNOUT TRAINING MANUAL

FOOT DRILL
Lesson 15

CHANGE STEP in quick time

A new Drill & Turnout Training manual has been created for the ACS21 syllabus to ensure streamlined teaching and to empower CFAVs by providing them with extra support to instruct cadets in drill.

'We've simplified the syllabus, removing elements that are no longer used, and sequencing lessons in a way that makes more sense,' says Jack.

'We've also increased the support provided to CFAVs with videos and learning resources. The manual has also been designed to be read comfortably on a phone or tablet.'

What's in the Army Cadets Drill & Turnout Training Manual?

- Foot drill
- Rifle exercises
- Banner drill
- The pace-stick
- Turnout
- Annexes including aids to drill, words of command, time and pace, and notes for inspecting officers

Fieldcraft &
TACTICS

Getting camo'd up and taking part in fieldcraft activities is one of the most exciting elements of Army Cadets. To help cadets hone their skills, the new ACS21 syllabus has revised the Fieldcraft & Tactics training materials. We've cherrypicked some areas to swot up on, and reveal what the new manual contains.

1. Camouflage

Camouflage consists of disrupting the contrasts of shape, silhouette, texture and, to some extent, shadow, so cadets are less conspicuous in the field. Good camouflage allows cadets to see without being seen.

The tone and colour of the hands, neck and face, and the texture and silhouette of the head and pack, must not contrast with their backgrounds. To avoid contrasts:

- Put camouflage cream, mud, burnt cork or something similar on the face, neck and hands. Put more on for night work than for day as skin will appear brighter in dim light.

- String or elastic may be used on equipment such as helmets to hold foliage which will break up the outline. It is essential that access to equipment is not impaired and that there's freedom of movement.

- The rifle is coloured green and black, so extra camouflage should not be necessary.

2. Judging distance by appearance

The amount of visible detail of a cadet at various ranges gives a good indication of how far away they are.

100m	**200m**	**300m**	**400m**	**500m**	**600m**
Clear in all detail.	Clear in all detail, colour of skin and equipment identifiable.	Clear body outline, face, colour good, remaining detailed blurred.	Body outline clear, remaining detail blurred.	Body begins to taper, head becomes indistinct.	Body now wedge shaped, no head apparent.

3. Concealment

Concealment means making the best use of cover from view, without sacrificing the minimum required fields of fire. Obeying the following rules will help you conceal yourself.

Look round or through cover, rather than over it. If you're compelled to look over it, avoid breaking a straight line.

Make use of available shadow. Remember that when in the sun your own shadow is very conspicuous – and that shadows move with the sun.

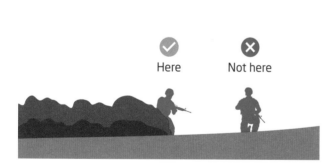

Avoid skylines

Avoid isolated cover as the enemy is likely to be observing it and it's easy to bring fire down on to this type of cover.

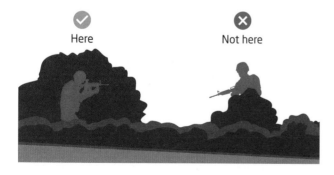

Choose a background to match the clothing and equipment being worn, so if you're wearing camouflage, trees and bushes provide good concealment.

172

4. Moving at night

A good enemy will always be alert at night, so it's important to know how to move at night without being detected. To move silently at night, cadets use the following 'walks'.

The Ghost Walk

Lift the leg high to avoid long grass and sweep it outwards. Feel gently with the toe for a safe place to put the foot down. Place the outside of the foot down prior to placing the whole foot down. Make sure one foot is providing firm support before moving the other. Keep the knees slightly bent. Carry the weapon as normal.

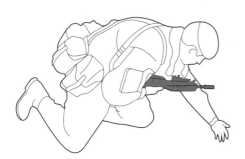

The Cat Walk

Crawl on hands and knees. Search the ground ahead for twigs with the left hand. The weapon is supported by the sling and held in the right hand. Move the knees up to the left hand and search again.

The Kitten Crawl

Lie on the stomach and search the ground ahead for twigs with the left hand. The weapon is supported by the sling and held in the right hand. To move forward, lift the body on forearms and toes, press it forward, then lower slowly. It is slow, quiet and tiring but ideal when it is necessary to get very close to an enemy position.

What's in the new Fieldcraft & Tactics Training Manual?

- Fieldcraft
- Tactics
- Exercises
- Cadet Force Tactical Aide Memoire

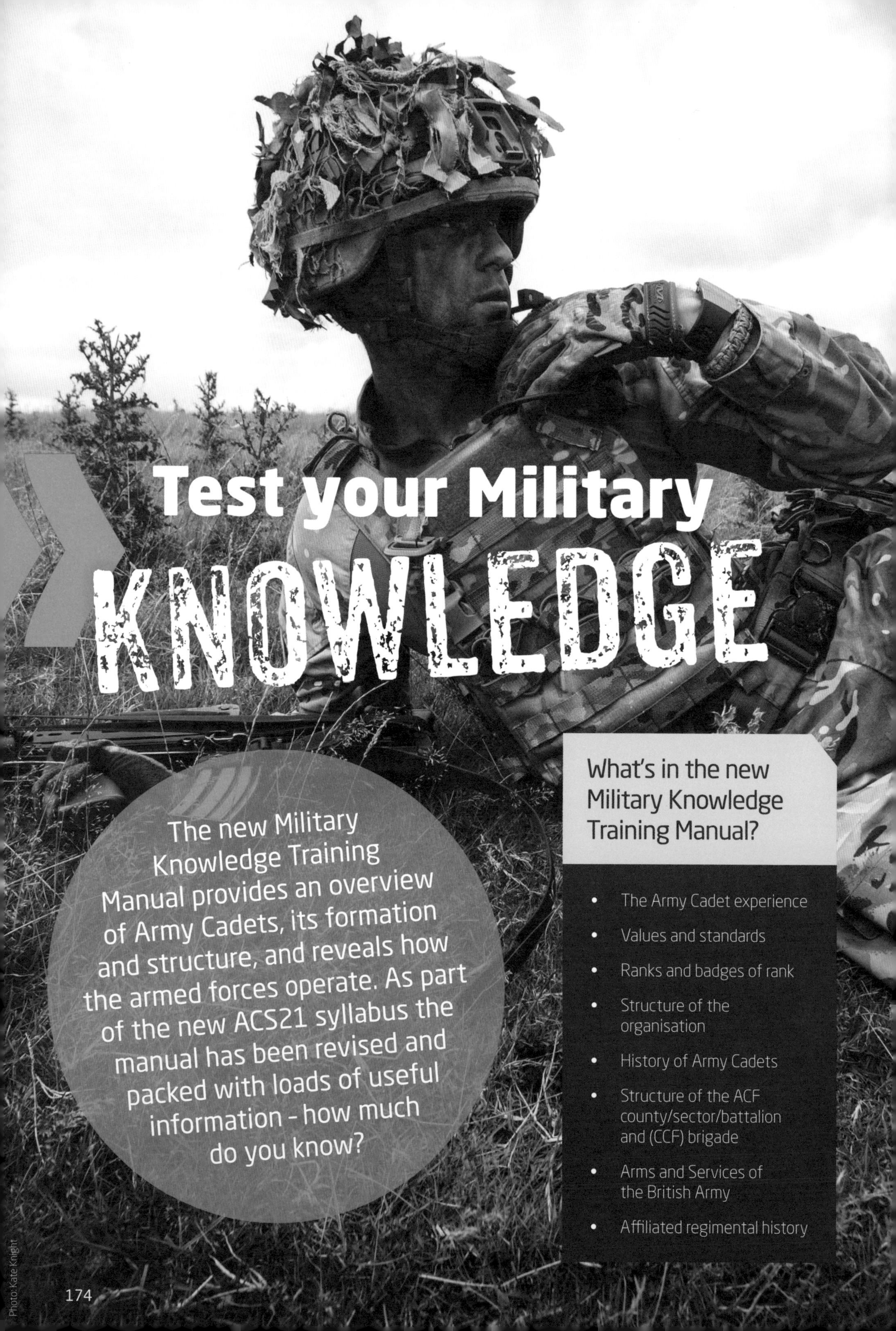

Test your Military KNOWLEDGE

The new Military Knowledge Training Manual provides an overview of Army Cadets, its formation and structure, and reveals how the armed forces operate. As part of the new ACS21 syllabus the manual has been revised and packed with loads of useful information – how much do you know?

What's in the new Military Knowledge Training Manual?

- The Army Cadet experience
- Values and standards
- Ranks and badges of rank
- Structure of the organisation
- History of Army Cadets
- Structure of the ACF county/sector/battalion and (CCF) brigade
- Arms and Services of the British Army
- Affiliated regimental history

Photo: Kate Knight

Think you've got the bases covered when it comes to Military Knowledge? Take the quick quiz and see how you do.

❶ How many of these **cadet badges** can you identify?

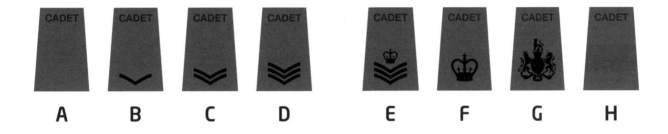

A   B   C   D   E   F   G   H

❷ Army Cadets uses **acronyms** – shorthand to make communication speedy and effective. How many do you know?

Term	Definition
ACF	Army Cadet Force
AI	Adult Instructor
CCF	Combined Cadet Force
CFAV	Cadet Force Adult Volunteer
CTT	Cadet Training Team
DC	Detachment Commander
DLE	Defence Learning Environment
DofE	Duke of Edinburgh's Award
HQ	Headquarters
NCO	Non-Commissioned Officer
NUV	Non-Uniformed Volunteers
OC	Officer Commanding
RFCA	Reserve Forces' and Cadets' Association
RPoC	Regional Point of Command

❸ British Army knowledge

A. The Army is organised into two key areas. What are they?

B. What does the acronym REME stand for?

C. Which corps is responsible for developing and maintaining physical fitness across the Army so individuals and units are prepared for military tasks?

D. What does the Military Provost Guard Service (MPGS) do?

Answers

1. Cadet badges
A. Cadet (Cdt)
B. Cadet Lance Corporal (Cdt LCpl)
C. Cadet Corporal (Cdt Cpl)
D. Cadet Sergeant (Cdt Sgt)
E. Cadet Staff Sergeant (Cdt SSgt)
F. Cadet Sergeant Major (Cdt SM)
G. Cadet Regimental Sergeant Major (Cdt RSM)
H. Cadet Under Officer (Cdt UO)

3. British Army Knowledge
A. Arms and Services
B. Corps of Royal Electrical and Mechanical Engineers
C. The Royal Army Physical Training Corps (RAPTC)
D. Provides trained professional soldiers to meet Defence armed security requirements

AT expeditions are back in ACTION!

After 18 months of restrictions, Adventurous Training expeditions are back. **Paul Randall** of The Ulysses Trust provides the low-down.

» What is The Ulysses Trust?

The Ulysses Trust works to ensure Adventurous Training (AT) is accessible and affordable.

The charity provides funding assistance to members of the Volunteer Reserve Forces and Cadet Forces in the UK who undertake challenging expeditions and adventurous activities.

It takes into account where units are based, how many cadets claim free school meals, whether participants are from single-parent families and if there is high unemployment in the area. It can also advise units on avenues to explore for possible grants.

Photo: Scot-Paddle Loch Shiel Southern Area Sea Cadets – Paddlesport Team

Photo: K ACF Glasgow Sport 2019 2nd NI Bn ACF

'2022 is set to be an exciting year for expeditions'

Photo: Scot-Paddle Loch Shiel Southern Area Sea Cadets – Paddlesport Team

» What AT can cadets look forward to in 2022?

2022 is set to be an exciting year for AT expeditions. While most are still in the planning stages, here are a few confirmed trips The Ulysses Trust is supporting:

Skiing Cadets, Glasgow and Lanarkshire Bn ACF

This expedition to Salzburger Sportwelt in Austria will introduce 28 cadets from Glasgow and Lanarkshire Bn ACF to the challenge and excitement of downhill skiing.

Scottish Mist, Somerset ACF

Cadets from Somerset ACF will travel to northern Scotland for a five-day canoeing and walking expedition from Fort William to Inverness. Two groups (who will carry all their own equipment and food for the expedition) will complete the Great Glen Way – one team on foot and the other by canoe.

» What's the best way to prepare for an expedition?

Whether it's their first or third AT expedition, cadets and adult volunteers need to prepare themselves in advance – both physically and mentally.

Cadets and adult volunteers should familiarise themselves with the equipment they'll be using and develop an appropriate level of technical skills prior to the expedition. This will be entirely dependent on the type of activity being undertaken. In some cases it might be nothing more than developing an appropriate level of fitness to ensure participants can enjoy the experience, rather than it being a slog.

AT instructors brief cadets in advance of the trip, giving them direction on what equipment they'll be using and the level of physical fitness required.

GO FURTHER »
Scan here to find out more
or visit ulyssestrust.co.uk

» #NoFilter goes national

A hugely successful Army Cadets recruitment drive, piloted in Surrey from February to April, started its nationwide roll-out in August.

Designed to encourage more cadets and adult volunteers to join Army Cadets, the #NoFilter Campaign used an assortment of eye-catching imagery with bold and engaging captions. The high-profile advertising campaign included the use of billboards, bus shelters, local radio, magazine adverts and social media.

The message of the recruitment drive was a simple but powerful one: while screens are great, they're no substitute for the cadet experience of fun, friendship, action, adventure and community. The images and

words drove home the message that people, places and skills are best experienced in real life.

Following the Surrey campaign, the recruitment drive launched in Wales and is now being expanded across the UK, including Scotland and Northern Ireland.

The aim is to encourage people to visit the Army Cadets website, show the benefits of joining Army Cadets, draw attention to the fantastic development opportunities for adult volunteers and demonstrate the benefits Army Cadets provides to the wider community.

Joanna Simpson of the Army Cadets media and comms team said: *'Almost immediately after*

the start of the Surrey campaign, Surrey ACF began to see a significant rise in the number of enquiries. After just one week, 30 young people completed their paperwork to join as cadets.

'Overall, Surrey ACF received well over 100 enquiries – many of which have, or are in the process of being, converted to members – while data from social media and online advertising shows there were 198 cadet and 67 adult volunteer applications by the end of the campaign period.

'We're really excited to watch the campaign roll out nationally and look forward to seeing an increase in membership and greater public engagement with Army Cadets.'

» Cadets join Jordan Wylie's polar challenge

Cadets joined Army Cadets National Ambassador Jordan Wylie in Running Dangerously: The Polar Edition by taking part in his virtual Pole to Pole challenge throughout August.

Cadets, CFAVs and family members were encouraged to set a target distance or fundraising amount and run or walk to hit their goal. Their activity was tracked via a leaderboard on the fundraising page as they competed against each other.

The challenge raised money for the Matthew Bacon Bursary Fund and the Army Cadet Charitable Trust (ACCT UK) – formerly known as the Army Cadet Force Association. This national charity is dedicated to improving the life chances of young people through access to Army Cadets.

Roger and Maureen Bacon set up the bursary in 2007 with the trust after their son, Intelligence Corps Officer and former cadet, Major Matthew Bacon lost his life in Iraq in 2005.

Jordan said: 'As well as keeping Matthew's memory alive, this inspiring project provides hope and the opportunity for adventure. It is an amazing initiative.'

Jordan Wylie is no stranger to adventure and one of his upcoming challenges will see him journey across the Arctic and Antarctic Oceans to run marathons on the North and South Poles.

Photo: Stephen McGrath

Summer reading

Lieutenant Colonel Mike Gerrish (rtd) wrote a memoir about his cadet experiences. The book, *60 Years a Cadet*, covered Mike's time as a young cadet, through his years as an officer with Northumberland ACF, to setting up the Cadet Adventure Centre and his civilian role in the Air Training Corps. To purchase a copy, email **edenhills16@gmail.com** £7.49 (plus £3 p&p).

» New warrant for Sergeant Major Instructors

A new warrant presented to CFAVs promoted to the rank of Sergeant Major Instructor (SMI) was introduced in August. The Cadet Forces Warrant recognised the value the MOD places on our senior non-commissioned CFAVs and the enormous effort required to reach this rank.

The warrant was agreed by the Secretary of State for Defence, the Rt Hon Ben Wallace MP, and issued to all current and future SMIs from 17 August.

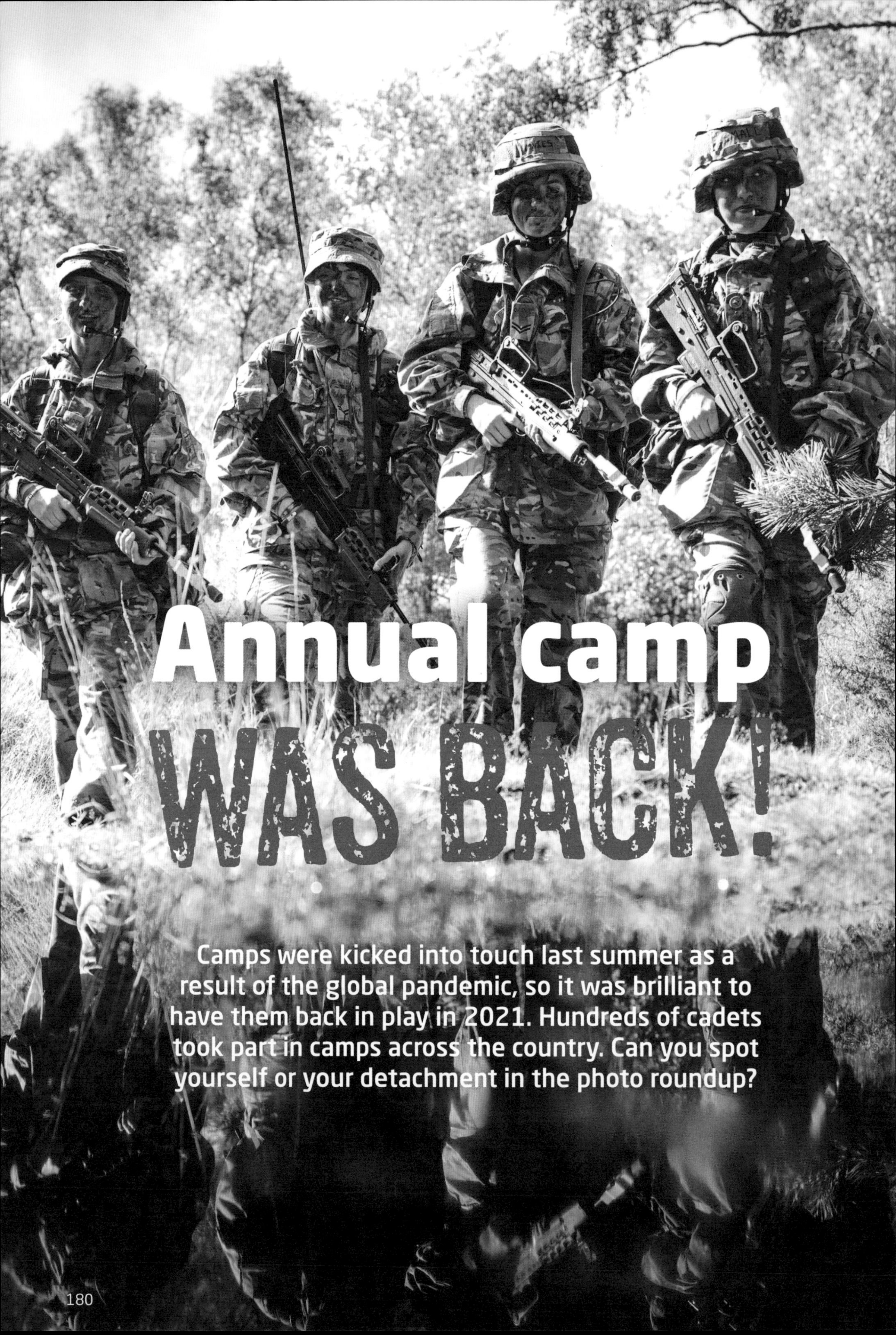

Annual camp
WAS BACK!

Camps were kicked into touch last summer as a result of the global pandemic, so it was brilliant to have them back in play in 2021. Hundreds of cadets took part in camps across the country. Can you spot yourself or your detachment in the photo roundup?

» **CCF 11X summer camp at Longmoor**

1

2

3

4

Hampshire and Isle of Wight ACF senior cadets patrolling during a field exercise on annual camp
Photo: Kate Knight

1 Cadets relax after a free-play paintballing activity **2** Cadets having fun on the water
3 Enjoying the survival stand **4** Training in Built-Up Areas (TIBUA)

Photos: Kate Knight

Annual camp
WAS BACK!

1

2

3

4

5

6

To Inspire To Achieve

1 Senior cadet applying camouflage cream 2 Senior cadets ready for the field exercise 3 SI J Harris during the field exercise
4 Senior cadets receiving quick battle orders during field exercise 5 Senior cadets post-exercise with the objective
6 Barossa Company cadets dealing with a casualty evacuation scenario during field exercise 7 Senior cadets receiving an
orders group during field exercise Photos: Kate Knight 8 Normandy Company cadet learning first aid Photo: PI Peter Davies
9 Gallipoli Company cadet with shotgun during Adventurous Training 10 Cadets on climbing wall during Adventurous
Training 11 Cambrai Company cadet shooting with Army Cadets National Ambassador Jordan Wylie Photos: SMI Karen Toze

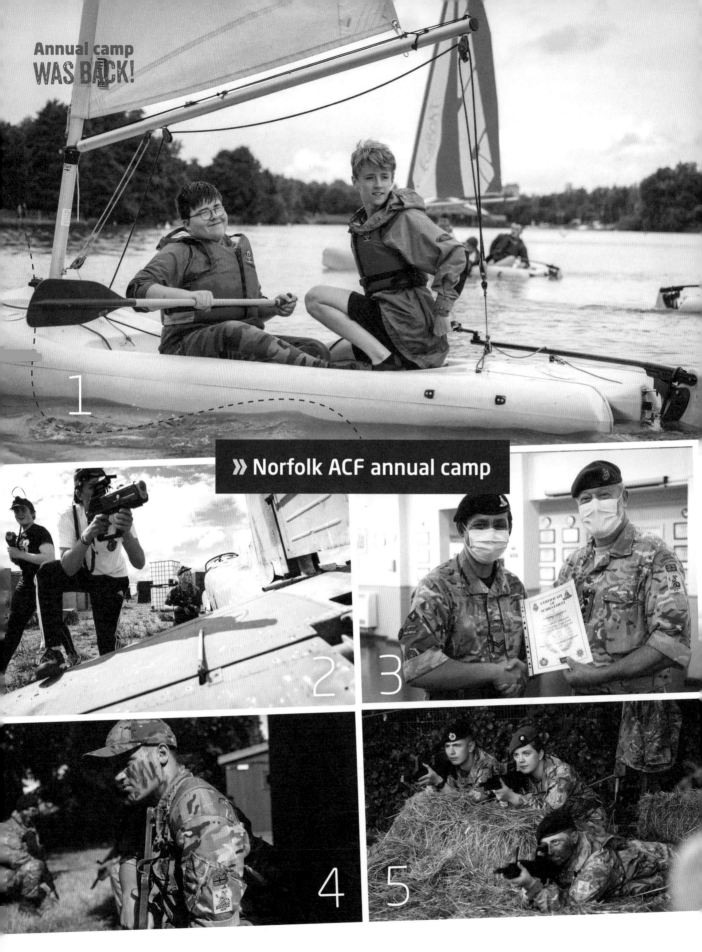

Annual camp
WAS BACK!

1

» Norfolk ACF annual camp

2 3

4 5

1 Britannia Company sailing on Whitlingham Broad, Norwich **2** Cadets practise their fire and manoeuvre skills via laser tag
3 Corporal Bishop from Britannia Company passes his Junior Cadet Instructor Course and is awarded a certificate by Norfolk ACF Commandant
Colonel Malin at Dereham **4 & 5** Cadets refresh their knowledge of basic through to 1-star fieldcraft at Dereham Photos: Kate Knight

To Inspire To Achieve

» Cambridgeshire ACF annual camp

1 Cadet Corporal Revelo tries on an army helmet at a Royal Anglian Recruiting stand, alongside Army Cadets Champion 'Big Phil' Campion and a soldier of The Royal Anglian Regiment **2** Captain Tom Knights and Major James Wood complete Weapons Handling Tests under the supervision of SSI Dale Irving **3** Cadet Elliot Lawson of 3 Coy Cambridgeshire ACF celebrates a win in the laser tag games **4** Cadets from 2 Coy Cambridgeshire ACF on motorbikes **5** Cadet Corporal Leah Scott from Newmarket detachment and fellow cadets canoeing **6** Cadets from 3 Coy Cambridgeshire ACF after taking part in laser tag

Photos: PI Doug Stuart

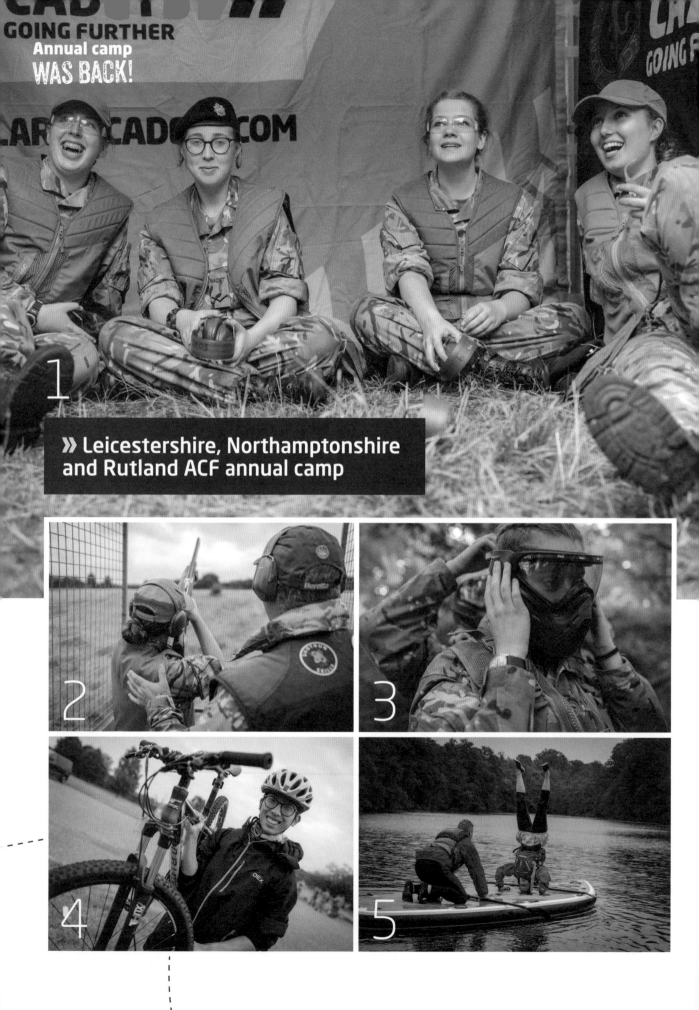

GOING FURTHER
Annual camp
WAS BACK!

» **Leicestershire, Northamptonshire and Rutland ACF annual camp**

1

2

3

4

5

To Inspire To Achieve

6

7

9

8

1 Cadets enjoying downtime while waiting to go on the shotgun range 2 CFAV supports a cadet using a shotgun 3 Cadet checks facial PPE of another before paintball 4 Cadet after bike checks and before hitting the cycle trail 5 CFAV proves a 10-person SUP is stable enough for yoga 6 Cadets taking part in archery 7 Cadet practising navigational skills 8 Camp was different this year, with time for cadets to just be together and make lifelong friends 9 Smiles after a 36-hour Fieldcraft exercise

Photos: Kate Knight

Annual camp
WAS BACK!

» CCF South West annual camp at Yoxter

1 Cadets hit the mark during archery practice
2 Cadets reach new heights on the climbing wall
3 Teamwork makes the dream work
4 Smiles on annual camp

Photos: Kate Knight

» Clwyd and Gwynedd ACF annual camp

1

2

3

4

1 'Big Phil' Campion visits cadets on summer camp and chats to them lakeside at Llyn Padarn, Llanberis 2 & 3 Phil joins cadets on the water 4 Cadet Dylan Williams of Penygroes Detachment with Phil at a presentation at Kinmel Park Camp (Dylan is receiving Best Map Keeper on the Minden Company navigation day)

Photos: John Baxendale, Clwyd & Gwynedd ACF

» Farewell to Colonel Clint Riley

At the end of September 2021 Clint Riley stepped down from his position as ACF Colonel Cadets.

Speaking of Colonel Clint's departure, Brigadier Stuart Williams OBE said: *'Clint Riley is the embodiment of this organisation. He has been involved with Army Cadets for over 46 years and I can think of no better person to have been the first ACF Colonel Cadets. In his tenure, he has established this post and selflessly championed the organisation far and wide, inspiring thousands of volunteers to commit to providing opportunities and life skills for our young people.*

'The ACF family owes Clint a deep debt of gratitude.'

'The ACF family owes Clint a deep debt of gratitude'

Army Cadets National Ambassador Jordan Wylie, Army Cadets National Honorary Colonel Lorraine Kelly and ACF Colonel Cadets Clint Riley

» Arthur's walk for heroes

Cadet Arthur Mortimer, 15, of Warwickshire and West Midlands (South Sector) ACF was featured in his local paper, the *Rugby Advertiser* after raising over £6K for veterans.

Arthur and his dad Kevin undertook a gruelling 150-mile march from Old Laurentians RFC in Rugby, Warwickshire to Arthur's grandparents' home in Llanhilleth, South Wales. The pair set out to raise £500 for Help for Heroes. However, at time of writing, their total stands at an astonishing £6,217.

» Remembrance resources

As 2021 was the Royal British Legion's centennial year, Army Cadets revisited our national Remembrance traditions.

The Royal British Legion, in partnership with Army Cadets and the National Literacy Trust, created an engaging set of new learning resource for cadets, enabling them to explore what Remembrance means and how they can help shape its future.

Activities, photographs, illustrations, videos and voices of cadets, past and present, will help bring Remembrance to life. To access the resources visit www.britishlegion.org.uk

Photo: Charlotte Graham Photography

» The world's toughest row

Four members of the Royal Army Physical Training Corps – Captain Scott Pollock, Warrant Officer Victoria Blackburn, Staff Sergeant Phillip Welch and Sergeant Laura Barrigan – will take up this year's brutal Talisker Whisky Atlantic Challenge.

In December 2021, the Force Atlantic team will tackle what has been billed 'the world's toughest row': an unsupported 3,000-mile race across the North Atlantic in an 8.5m boat.

They'll spend six weeks rowing in gruelling two-hour shifts – day and night – as they battle their way from La Gomera in the Canary Islands to the beaches of Antigua.

The primary aim of the challenge is to highlight the many opportunities that exist in the Army, regardless of gender, social class or level of sporting ability. Read more at www.forceatlantic.com

» One Run Global Relay

Army Cadets supported One Run Global Relay, a worldwide event where thousands of people – including Army Cadets National Ambassador Sally Orange (pictured) – from the world's 195 countries took part in an epic relay across 24 hours.

The run took place on 16 October 2021. Find out how it went at onerun.global – or scan the QR code.

Cadets, camera, ACTION!

Adventurer and Army Cadets National Ambassador **Jordan Wylie** is making an exciting new documentary about Army Cadets. He tells us about the project.

Jordan Wylie is thrilled to be casting a spotlight on our organisation in a new TV documentary, *Inside the Army Cadets,* in which he visits counties across the UK to talk to cadets and CFAVs.

'One of my main roles for Army Cadets is to make sure everyone in the UK knows who we are, what we do and the value we bring to society,' he says. *'We're the nation's best-kept secret so I felt a documentary would reveal the inspiring people involved in our organisation and the amazing opportunities available to everyone.'*

Manchester's Standby Productions has been commissioned to produce the documentary and there's already a huge buzz around the project.

'It's been a real eye opener for me and the production team to meet so many inspiring people, and we are encouraging all detachments to reach out to us to share stories and experiences,' he says.

Photos: Kate Knight

» Keeping it real

Far from trying to create a glossy promotional film, Jordan is aiming for an authentic insight into what Army Cadets life is all about and to dispel any myths.

'People can sometimes have preconceived ideas about those who wear uniforms, perhaps even more so when the attire is similar to the armed forces.

'I hope to show people we are simply an inspiring youth organisation which happens to be sponsored by the MOD. This allows us many benefits and opportunities, such as access to their adventure training centres and some of the best leadership and team-building programmes in the world, along with a whole host of other perks, including a very smart uniform.

'I think people will be very surprised at what they see, especially the opportunities – some of which can't be found anywhere else in the world.'

'I felt a documentary would reveal the inspiring people involved in our organisation'

» Hunting fugitives

Jordan is no stranger to filming and TV, and is a familiar face on Channel 4's *Hunted* and *Celebrity Hunted*. As one of the elite group of hunters, he's tasked with tracking down people who are on the run. His tips for hunting fugitives?

'I wouldn't be a good hunter if I gave away trade secrets, but I can say that every time we use a social media app of some sort, we leave a trail of data for others. Every time we pass a CCTV camera, someone is capturing our movements. Every time we spend money using a card, we leave a scent which the team and I can close in on. Sometimes the best plan a fugitive can have is not to have a plan at all.'

Despite this TV work, Jordan's biggest passion is the world of adventure: exploring new places, meeting new people and making a positive impact on the next generation.

'If I am completely honest, I don't watch much TV and I don't take being on TV too seriously. The best part about it is using the profile it gives me to help charities and important causes off screen. Being on TV comes with lots of benefits but it should come with great responsibility too.'

» Advice for tough times

Since leaving the military, Jordan has experienced lows as well as highs: he's battled depression, anxiety and, more recently, epilepsy. He now campaigns to remove the stigma from people suffering with mental illness.

'We all face challenges in our life – physical and mental – and I'm no different. We need to talk to others to help fix our problems and we need to take ownership of whatever it is we are going through – which means acknowledging there is a problem in the first place.

'I find the great outdoors one of the best medicines and not to be underestimated.'

» Astonishing achievements

Jordan's CV is inspiring. The former soldier became the first person to row solo across the Bab Al Mandeb Strait between the Horn of Africa and Yemen, which is often described as the most dangerous stretch of water on the planet. His Running Dangerously project saw him run through Somalia, Afghanistan and Iraq, all countries he has previously worked or served in. He's also climbed Mount Kilimanjaro – completely barefoot.

His exploits have raised over a million pounds for charity and been featured in TV documentaries. During lockdown, he managed to spend longer on a stand-up paddleboard than anyone had ever done before.

'The last 12 months have been a huge rollercoaster of emotions. I was very privileged to have spent 149 days on a paddleboard attempting to circumnavigate Great Britain in a world record attempt, but this was abruptly halted by Covid-19. It was one of the toughest challenges I have ever taken on, especially crossing the Irish Sea and rounding Cape Wrath in winter.'

Jordan taking a winter dip in the freezing cold waters of Diamond Beach, Iceland, after completing another one of his incredible Running Dangerously marathons

Photo: Stephen McGrath

'I find the great outdoors one of the best medicines'

» Up for a challenge

Jordan is never afraid to try new things and has this advice for cadets:

'Pursue the things you enjoy. When you stop enjoying what you do, move on to something else or try something new. Education is important but that doesn't have to mean sitting in a classroom or passing exams. I learn just as much when I'm climbing, paddling, running and challenging myself in a new environment.

'Your attitude is the most important thing. If you have a positive, can-do approach to life, people will always give you a chance and you'll get to wherever it is you wish to be in this world.'

Jordan's next challenge comes in the form of heading to Antarctica and the North Pole in his quest to run extreme marathons in the coldest climates on earth. With his can-do attitude, we've no doubt he'll pull it off.

» Jordan's A B C rules for life

Attitude determines your altitude: stay positive and aim for the highest peaks.

Building relationships everywhere you go is how opportunities are formed.

Continuous professional development: never stop learning as you progress through life.

Inside The Army Cadets is currently in production and, in addition to possible TV screening, will be available via YouTube and Army Cadets channels – see social media channels for details.

Behind the scenes at
SANDHURST

It takes 44 weeks of intensive training to produce a soldier worthy of the position of one of Her Majesty's Commissioned Officers, but what does that entail? Two newly commissioned officers from Royal Military Academy Sandhurst (RMAS) reveal insights into day-to-day life at the academy.

**Claudia Helen Wright,
26, Lieutenant,
Royal Signals**

What tips do you have for anyone facing the Army Officer Selection Board?

Practise the aptitude tests. People have this misconception that entry is based purely on your raw intelligence but it's not. You can, and should, practise. The best way to do this is to get the practice UKCAT tests used by those wishing to study medicine.

What got you through the hard times?

I struggled with motivation when I didn't fully achieve what I wanted in a few of the exercises. I'd set myself unrealistic targets and, in my eyes, this led to me failing. What got me through was the people in my platoon who reignited my spark so I wasn't surviving, but thriving.

You feel tired 90 per cent of the time and that's okay. Everyone else will be feeling the same so it's important not to let it get you down; everyone copes differently with fatigue.

What's life on camp like?

It's very structured. You get used to it pretty quickly as you don't have any choice. After waking up at 5am to do block jobs, you're then on the line singing the national anthem at 6am. Then it's breakfast and into your working day of lessons. As you progress through the terms (Junior to Intermediate to Senior) you gain more free time. You soon get used to marching everywhere and the protocol around which routes you can and can't take.

What was the most important lesson you learnt?

To trust myself. Officers have to make choices that impact soldiers, so we need to trust ourselves and trust that the training we've been given will guide us into making reasonable decisions.

Your best insider tips?

Prepare. Use time before you enrol to understand the different cap badges as this will make life a lot easier at the Regimental Selection Board.

Figure out what you want to do in the Army. RMAS is heavily orientated towards Infantry training and quite often people get bogged down focusing on that element.

Ironing Board Sunday (arrival day) will be one of the most nerve-racking days of your life and so will Regimental Selection Board, but relax – they are the start of a fantastic ride. Enjoy RMAS and remember US gymnast Simone Biles' mantra: look after your mental health as you don't owe anyone anything.

2 Lt Eleanor Potter, 24, is with the Vikings, the first battalion of the Royal Anglians deployed in Cyprus

Was the training a big step up from Army Cadets?

Being part of the CCF at school prepared me for my time at Sandhurst as I already had an enthusiasm for learning new skills and working as part of a team – both key to being an officer in the British Army.

It's definitely a step up, though, as when you get to Sandhurst you're working towards leading soldiers in challenging and potentially dangerous situations. It's not something to be scared of, as the challenge is manageable and the whole experience incredibly rewarding.

What did you find tough?

The sheer amount of new things you have to learn. I got through it by reminding myself that Sandhurst is a training environment – you're there to learn. All the staff want you to do well and achieve. You just need to have the humility to ask for help when you need it.

What did you enjoy most?

Learning something new every day. I was always being exposed to new facts, experiences and ways of looking at the world. That was why I wanted to join the British Army.

What was the food like?

You eat in a large dining hall or "scoff house" as it's known. From day one you sit and eat every meal with your platoon. There are lots of options for every meal, and you also get NERTS which are snacks to keep you going overnight – you do a lot of physical training and need the extra food.

What did you learn about yourself?

That it's important to maintain a sense of humour and a positive mental attitude. Everything that seems hard will come to an end and you'll always reach the top of the hill. Having a sense of humour when times get tough stands you in good stead for your career and is an excellent attribute to have as an officer.

Was it easy to make new friends?

Quite easy as the range of people there is hugely diverse. However, I think it's important to know that not everyone will get along all the time; you're operating in what can be a high-stress environment. That is all part of the training.

I made good friends at Sandhurst who I trust and respect, and who I could call on for advice if needed.

Your best insider tips?

Be yourself from the get-go. You eat, breathe and sleep with the people around you, so if you're putting on an act you'll eventually be found out. And be a team player: the person you help today may be the person you need help from tomorrow.

⌄ Go further

The Royal Military Academy Sandhurst (RMAS) is where all officers in the British Army are trained to take on the responsibility of leading their soldiers. During training, officer cadets learn to live by the academy's motto: Serve to Lead.

The RMAS Youth Engagement Team are involved in exploring the Army's Values-Based Leadership, helping young people become the best they can be by exploring how self-awareness and lived values are vital for teamwork, leadership and employability.

This knowledge develops confidence and resilience in young people, supporting whatever career path they follow. The RMAS team hold events for cadets and other young people, teachers, parents and youth leaders. Contact them at **engagement@dgw365. onmicrosoft.com**

Beneath the BERET

Meet members of the Army Cadets family and find out how they support the organisation.

James Fraser
Training Safety Advisor, 1st Bn The Highlanders ACF

» Tell us about your role

My job is to ensure a safe system of training is in place and to give assurance to Regional Command that activities are being conducted as per guidelines. This covers many things including safeguarding on an expedition, ensuring the correct ratio of supervisors are on a range and giving support to CFAVs.

I'm not here to tell people what they can and can't do: I simply give advice and guidance on policy using my experience and training.

» What did you do before you joined Army Cadets?

I was in the Army for 25 years. I joined in 1996 and trained at Glencorse Barracks in Edinburgh, which also happened to be where I finished my career in 2020.

I spent nine and a half years of my military career working in training environments in positions such as Corporal Instructor at

Infantry Training Centre (ITC) Catterick and Instructor at the Infantry Battle School. My final role was at the Infantry Battle School as Divisional Sergeant Major (Master Coach) with the Platoon Commanders' Division.

I've taught every rank of the British Army: from private and corporal to platoon commander and sergeant.

» Were you a cadet?

No. Before I started my role in the ACF I never took the time to engage with it, which was a failing on my behalf. A lot of the soldiers I had with me in Iraq, Afghanistan and Northern Ireland were former cadets and were some of the best I worked with.

When I retired from the Army, I knew I had something I could offer the ACF and wanted to help make training enjoyable, memorable and safe.

'The opportunity to highland dance with Her Majesty The Queen as her Guard Sergeant Major at Balmoral'

James at Balmoral with Her Majesty The Queen

» The most exciting moment?

Having the opportunity – twice – to highland dance with Her Majesty The Queen as her Guard Sergeant Major at Balmoral.

» What's been the scariest moment of your career?

As a private soldier it was the presence of the unknown. When I was a senior NCO on tour as a platoon commander it was the knowledge that you are only ever a round away from not achieving your intent.

» Your proudest achievement?

My immediate thought was when I served as a platoon commander on an operational tour of Afghanistan in 2008. However, on reflection, I think it's been helping others; it's amazing watching people develop and reach their potential.

James' top tips for cadets

1. Listen to CFAVs. If you don't, you won't be policy compliant and things can go wrong.

2. Adhere to guidance and direction. CFAVs are there because they know what's best for cadets – they've done the training and have the experience.

3. Know your environment before your sprint. Whenever you begin a new lesson or exercise think: walk, jog, run, then sprint. This will build through your career and by the time you're a senior cadet you'll be sprinting into everything.

Beneath the BERET

Meet members of the Army Cadets family and find out how they support the organisation.

Shirley Montgomery
1st (Northern Ireland) Bn C Coy CVQO & PR Officer, Bn STEM Ambassador and CF National iDEA Awards Advisor

» Tell us about your role

I like to keep busy: within 1st (NI) Battalion, my primary role is Detachment Instructor with Cambridge House Grammar School in Ballymena (where I live). Other roles include CVQO and PR officer for C Company, and Treasurer for the Battalion Officers' Mess.

As Battalion STEM Ambassador, I help to integrate science, technology, engineering and mathematics into Army Cadet activities in interactive and enjoyable ways. Additionally, I'm a 38X First Aid Trainer as well as a Westminster Training Support Officer.

The National Cadet Forces iDEA Awards Advisor is a relatively new position where I champion a fantastic online resource which teaches valuable digital skills (more on that later).

» How did you become involved in Army Cadets?

There was no military influence in my family so I wasn't a cadet myself. However, I served for nine years as a Territorial Army volunteer with the 74 Royal Engineers (V). Then, in 2013, I kept seeing adverts on Facebook for female instructors for the ACF and I thought: *I could do that. I'm an engineer, I'm female and I've got a little bit of military background. I think I can make myself useful.* I commissioned in 2015 – and subsequently my partner and daughter followed me into Army Cadets.

» What are the highlights?

It can be hard work – anyone involved in Army Cadets knows it soaks up every second you allow it to take – but seeing the achievements of the cadets is phenomenal. It's so gratifying to see young people achieve things they could never have dreamt of even attempting.

There is a huge sense of belonging and camaraderie fostered in the Cadets, and it's most evident when you come back from annual camp. The cadets are devastated to leave and there are always tears at the docks when we get back to Belfast. It's a sight to behold.

» Proudest achievements?

I was the first person in Northern Ireland to be offered – and complete – the Initial Officer Training Programme (IOT). In the process I was given the Tutor's Award for my syndicate, of which I'm immensely proud.

I also received a Brigade Commander's Coin in 2018 for my STEM work and was notified that I'm being given an Army Cadet Force Certificate of Good Service. It comes from Regional Command HQ – I was fairly shocked when I found out.

Shirley receiving the Brigade Commander's Coin with her daughter Carrie Morrow

» Tell us about STEM

In 2018 the British Army launched a Year of Engineering campaign, and STEM became a huge focus for Army Cadets. The skills are vital across all elements of the cadet syllabus – from first aid through to navigation and fieldcraft.

The first Army Cadets STEM camp took place in 2016. I've attended all the camps since 2017, including the virtual one. It was at camp in 2017 that Colonel Clint Riley introduced me to the iDEA Award which is inherently linked to the practical, problem-solving skills found in STEM subjects. I recommend it highly for all cadets and volunteers.

Go further

Follow Shirley for updates, help and support. Her (virtual) office door is always open.

f @CFiDEAadvisor

🐦 @CFiDEAadvisor

📷 @CFiDEAadvisor

✉ CFiDEAadvisor@armymail.mod.uk

iDEA Inspiring Digital Enterprise Award

What? iDEA is the digital equivalent of the Duke of Edinburgh's Award. It's a free platform which allows cadets and CFAVs to gain IT knowledge and skills. At Bronze (beginner) level, cadets earn points by achieving badges (content is broken down into bite-size chunks). There are 68 badges across five categories: Citizen, Worker, Maker, Entrepreneur and Gamer. There's a huge variety and it's completely up to the user which badges they try.

Why? It's estimated by iDEA that, within the next 20 years, 90 per cent of jobs will have a digital element. As cadets progress through the award, each of the badges earned – and the skills associated with it – are marked in a Record of Achievement. That's a cast-iron piece of evidence to take to interviews or put on a CV as evidence of skills and understanding of a variety of digital topics.

How? Visit the website and get going. It takes less than two minutes to sign up and there's no time limit on completion, so cadets can dip in and out as they please.

Digital badge It's important that users identify themselves as a cadet or CFAV on their iDEA profile. This is done by adding the user's unit code to their profile (it must be the county code).

This element can be done even after achieving the award. Cadets working through the award at school can claim their digital ACF or CCF badge just by adding their cadet unit code.

Cadets can gain all sorts of digital expertise with iDEA badges, for example: social media and business, junior web designer, making a game, digital careers, user experience, crisis management.

Visit **www.idea.org.uk** to find out more.

Beneath the
BERET

Meet members of the Army Cadets family and find out how they support the organisation.

Ian Smith

Deputy Commandant Hampshire and Isle of Wight (based in Winchester)

» When did you become a cadet?

I joined the local ACF detachment in Winchester in 1974. It was a brand new venture within Montgomery of Alamein School, where I studied.

I went to see what it was about, along with 200 others, and straight away thought, *Yeah, I'm going to enjoy this*. Immediately after joining, I started the DofE and gained other skills through the Army Proficiency Certificate. It massively increased my confidence.

» What's your role in Army Cadets?

I oversee cadet training for AT, DofE and CIS.

» How has Army Cadets changed during your 46 years' service?

Today, young people have a confidence they didn't have ten years ago. Army Cadets can build on that and provide them with training, structure and discipline.

» What are the main benefits to young people?

It's the best feeling to see a 13-year-old, with no clue about life, age out at 18 as a proud and confident individual with a better understanding of society.

Army Cadets is a fun way for them to gain confidence and achieve their dreams; it sets them up for the rest of their life.

» What are the highlights?

Everything I do for Army Cadets is a highlight, although it does give you a bit of a buzz when royalty attends events, especially when you get to meet them.

My county ACF was part of the Princess of Wales' Royal Regiment (PWRR) ceremony when the Royal Hampshire Regiment formed part of the regiment. I got to meet the Princess – albeit briefly.

'It's the best feeling to see a 13-year-old, with no clue about life, age out at 18 as a proud and confident individual'

» Memorable moments?

Seeing all four of my sons join the ACF and perform with ACF Music at various locations around the UK – and even in front of royalty. That was probably something none of them ever dreamt of, but the Army Cadets provided the opportunity.

» What's your day job?

I'm a Defence Transport Manager and work at a military base in Winchester. My Army Cadets background helps me fit into my job and vice versa – my work environment helps me see how things work in the Cadets.

» Why would you recommend being a CFAV?

It enhances your skills and provides an overwhelming sense of pride as you watch young people gain experiences they would be unlikely to achieve in any other organisation. It's a privilege to see them all become better citizens.

Anyone thinking of joining this amazing organisation should go for it. They'll have the chance to inspire young people to become developed versions of themselves, and there's no better feeling than knowing you've helped them through difficult times.

» What would your ACF colleagues be surprised to learn about you?

I was a very shy boy with no confidence, and I am dyslexic. If it wasn't for Army Cadets, and the many cadets I have had the pleasure to instruct and mentor, I'd still be that shy individual.

⍖⍖ Beneath the
BERET

Meet members of the Army Cadets family and find out how they support our organisation.

Catherine Harrison
Commandant of Greater Manchester ACF since December 2020

⟫ Tell us about your role

I'm ultimately responsible for everything that takes place within Greater Manchester ACF.

I spend a lot of time talking with and listening to people within and outside the organisation, ensuring we retain a very clear focus on how we can improve the cadet experience, celebrate success and strengthen our position within the wider community of Greater Manchester.

⟫ Best and worst bits?

Being Commandant is such a privileged position and having the opportunity to influence progress and help others grow is probably the most rewarding part. However, it's true what they say about the loneliness of command, and as Commandant it sometimes feels I am no longer seen as an individual, but as the appointment. As someone who has grown up through the ACF and thrives in an environment of mutually trusting relationships, this is more of a challenge than I anticipated.

⟫ Key priorities?

My immediate priority is rebuilding Greater Manchester ACF after the pandemic. That means ensuring we have a respectful culture where adult volunteers feel genuinely supported and enthused about how they contribute to the cadet experience, and are enabled to provide safe, fun and rewarding training.

It's also important for us to proactively embrace the diversity of the communities we serve, and raise our collective and individual ambitions.

⟫ How do you feel as the first female in the role?

It's frustrating that we're still talking about the "first female" doing anything in the Army Cadets. So, while I am proud of this appointment, I also hope I'm one of a growing number of role models who, by their appointment, will remove limitations to equality by challenging stereotypes and unconscious bias.

Celebrating with Senior Padre, Rev Dr Gerard Fieldhouse-Byrne on the first day of annual camp and the first day back at Holcombe Moor with the cadets

» Were you a cadet?

Yes, I joined in 1989 in Bourton-on-the-Water Platoon, part of A Company, Gloucestershire ACF. I was hooked from day one.

I was losing interest in the Girl Guides so when the local Army Cadets instructors came in one evening to teach us navigation, I quickly jumped ship. I loved everything about Army Cadets and many of my closest friendships are those I made as a result of joining.

» How did being a cadet affect your life?

Army Cadets has certainly made me who I am today. I have a deep interest in the wellbeing of other people, leadership, teamwork and the achievement of shared goals. This has influenced my career choices and helped me work out what's important to me.

» What would we be surprised to learn about you?

I've been a season ticket holder at Manchester City FC since 2007. It's tricky to balance football matches and Cadets but where there's a will there's a way. I think people are surprised about this when they first meet me – perhaps it's not a traditional pastime of a County Commandant.

» Who has most inspired you?

My parents – for their hard work, community spirit and the value they put on simply living life.

Major Mick Little, one of my previous Company Commanders in Gloucestershire ACF, was also a real inspiration for many years. He taught me a lot about leadership and the importance of treating people fairly. I often frame my decisions around what I think he would have done.

» What's been your greatest achievement?

I'm extremely proud to have been part of the Army Cadets for 32 years and still have the same passion for it as on my first day. Recently, I met up with some former cadets and their families and to hear, even after so many years, that they consider me to have had a positive influence in their lives makes me very proud.

Cadet Forces MEDALS

The Cadet Forces Medal is awarded to commissioned officers and non-commissioned adult instructors of the UK Cadet Forces in recognition of long and efficient service. Clasps are issued for every six additional years. Huge congratulations to everyone included in this October 2020 to September 2021 round-up.

5TH CLASP

CAPT	B P	LUCAS	ACF	1st Bn Highlanders ACF
COL	A I	DENISON	ACF	HQ London District
MAJ	P D	HYDE	ACF	Humberside & South Yorkshire ACF
MAJ	K A	PICKERING	ACF	Norfolk ACF

4TH CLASP

MAJ	A R	MORRIS	ACF	Buckinghamshire (The Rifles) ACF
CAPT	C J	CHERRY	CCF	Colfe's School CCF, London
CAPT	R	BARRITT	ACF	Dorset ACF
CAPT	P	CROSS	ACF	Dyfed & Glamorgan ACF
MAJ	N	WARREN	ACF	Greater London South East Sector ACF
LT COL	P	SMILLIE	ACF	Greater Manchester ACF
CAPT	N W	EDMUNDS	ACF	Gwent & Powys ACF
MAJ	J P	HYDE	ACF	Hereford & Worcester ACF
SMI	S	BORTHWICK	ACF	Lothian & Borders Bn ACF
SSI	A K	SHERMAN	ACF	Oxfordshire (The Rifles) Bn ACF
COL	D M	STEELE	ACF	Sussex ACF
LT COL	G C	DEMPSEY	ACF	West Lowland Bn ACF

3RD CLASP

MAJ	C W	MILNE	ACF	2nd Bn The Highlanders ACF
CAPT	E A	MASSIE	CCF	Bedford School CCF Bedfordshire
MAJ	D R	OUTRAM	ACF	Bedfordshire & Hertfordshire ACF
SSI	G M	PRICE	ACF	Bedfordshire & Hertfordshire ACF
SMI	A	MACKENZIE	ACF	Cambridgeshire ACF
COL	M L	CRAVEN	ACF	Clwyd & Gwynedd ACF
LT	K W	RIDGMENT	ACF	Cornwall ACF
CAPT	M R	BAKER	ACF	Cornwall ACF
MAJ	D A	SWINBURNE	CCF	Cranbrook School CCF Kent
SMI	T J	BATES	ACF	Devon ACF
CAPT	D	MORRISON	ACF	Glasgow & Lanarkshire Bn ACF
SMI	S J	MULLOY	ACF	2nd Bn The Highlanders ACF
COL	C R	JONES	ACF	HQ SW London ACF
LT	N G	MACLEOD	CCF	Kelvinside Academy Glasgow
SMI	C W	PRIZEMAN	ACF	Kent ACF
MAJ	W J	TYRER	ACF	Lancashire ACF
SMI	J L	BITHELL	ACF	Leicestershire, Northamptonshire & Rutland ACF
SMI	D J	DANNANTT	ACF	Lincolnshire ACF
LT COL	M A	WATSON	ACF	Nottinghamshire ACF
SSI	A K	SHERMAN	ACF	Oxfordshire (The Rifles) Bn ACF
CAPT	A D	GODFREY	ACF	Oxfordshire (The Rifles) Bn ACF

SSI	J L B	SMITH	ACF	Oxfordshire (The Rifles) Bn ACF
MAJ	A P	WYNN	CCF	Royal Hospital School CCF Suffolk
MAJ	K	SYKES	CCF	Sandbach School Cheshire
MAJ	J G	KITCHING	ACF	Somerset ACF
SMI	S A	SHELLEY	ACF	Somerset ACF
MAJ	M C	GALLEY	ACF	Suffolk ACF
LT COL	G S	JUPP	ACF	Surrey ACF
LT COL	S S	SAUNDERSON	CCF	The Duke of York's Royal Military School Kent
LT COL	S A	OAKLEY	ACF	Royal County of Berkshire ACF
LT COL	G D	LOCK	CCF	Vyne School CCF Hampshire
LT	V A	BROOKHOUSE	ACF	Warwickshire & West Midlands (South Sector) ACF
CAPT	J P	CROOKES	CCF	Welbeck Defence Sixth Form College Leicestershire
MAJ	R P	NORMAN	CCF	Wellington School CCF Somerset
LT COL	G C	DEMPSEY	ACF	West Lowland Bn ACF
LT COL	P J	WHITE	ACF	Wiltshire ACF

2ND CLASP

SSI	M S	DONACHIE	ACF	1st Bn Highlanders ACF
SI	P J	STANDEN	ACF	1st Bn Highlanders ACF
MAJ	J	NEWMAN	ACF	2nd (Northern Ireland) Bn ACF
CAPT	J F	BROWN	ACF	Argyll & Sutherland Highlanders Bn ACF
SSI	R D	TEKELL-MELLOR	CCF	Bedford School CCF Bedfordshire
SMI	W G	McALLISTER	ACF	Bedfordshire & Hertfordshire ACF
MAJ	T G	ADAMS	ACF	Bedfordshire & Hertfordshire ACF
SMI	A A	DANE	ACF	City & County of Bristol ACF
SMI	I P	TRAVERS	ACF	City of London & North East Sector ACF
MAJ	D C	HOLMAN	ACF	Cornwall ACF
MAJ	D A	SWINBURNE	CCF	Cranbrook School CCF Kent
SMI	D	KIRKPATRICK	ACF	Cumbria ACF
MAJ	A	RICHMOND	ACF	Cumbria ACF
CAPT	K L	BARKER	ACF	Dorset ACF
SSI	S	CROUCH	ACF	Dorset ACF
RSMI	J	SAYERS	ACF	Durham ACF
LT	D	EVANS	ACF	Dyfed & Glamorgan ACF
COL	A	LAMB	CCF	Eastbourne College CCF East Sussex
CAPT	A D	HILL	ACF	Greater London South East Sector ACF
MAJ	A J	WHITE	ACF	Greater London South East Sector ACF
SSI	L J	BORAINE	ACF	Hampshire & IOW ACF
SMI	R I	KENT	ACF	Hampshire & IOW ACF
LT COL	W M A	LAND	CCF	Harrow School CCF Middlesex
SSI	C J	ROSE	CCF	Heles School Devon

To Inspire To Achieve

Rank	Initials	Surname	Org	Unit
SMI	P R	CHANDLER	ACF	Hereford & Worcester ACF
LT	N G	MACLEOD	CCF	Kelvinside Academy Glasgow
MAJ	V A	DAWKINS	ACF	Lancashire ACF
SSI	A C	INGLE	ACF	Leicestershire, Northamptonshire & Rutland ACF
MAJ	J P	MAYES	ACF	Leicestershire, Northamptonshire & Rutland ACF
2LT	E	RICHARDSON	ACF	Leicestershire, Northamptonshire & Rutland ACF
CAPT	P A	MACDONALD	ACF	Lothian & Borders Bn ACF
SMI	J	GILLISON	ACF	Merseyside ACF
CAPT	S C	LOFTS	ACF	Middlesex & North West London ACF
CAPT	C	ASHTON	ACF	Norfolk ACF
SMI	G R	MORRISON	ACF	Northumbria ACF
LT COL	A A	PUGH	ACF	Northumbria ACF
SSI	G D	WESSON	ACF	Nottinghamshire ACF
CAPT	I	MASON	ACF	Nottinghamshire ACF
CAPT	M I	ALLINGTON	ACF	Oxfordshire (The Rifles) Bn ACF
SSI	N O	GODFREY	ACF	Oxfordshire (The Rifles) Bn ACF
MAJ	S L	OXFORD	ACF	Oxfordshire (The Rifles) Bn ACF
SSI	P A	WELLS	CCF	Reeds School CCF Surrey
MAJ	G T	SCOBLE	CCF	Royal Grammar School CCF, Buckinghamshire
MAJ	K	SYKES	CCF	Sandbach School Cheshire
CAPT	S L	McTAGGART	ACF	Shropshire ACF
SSI	R H S	EDWARDS	ACF	Shropshire ACF
LT COL	A J	STEVENS	ACF	Shropshire ACF
LT	J G	KITCHING	ACF	Somerset ACF
SMI	N P	LEVETT	ACF	Somerset ACF
SMI	J	MURPHY	ACF	Somerset ACF
MAJ	K M	LORIMER	ACF	South West London ACF
MAJ	J M	SCRASE	ACF	Sussex ACF
RSMI	P	CAMERON	ACF	The Black Watch Bn ACF
MAJ	N A	MURDOCH	ACF	The Black Watch Bn ACF
LT COL	C A	THOMPSON	CCF	Thomas Deacon Academy CCF Cambridgeshire
MAJ	P	MAZUR	CCF	Trinity School CCF Surrey
CAPT	J P	CROOKES	CCF	Welbeck Defence Sixth Form College Leicestershire
CAPT	A	PHILPOTT	CCF	Wellington College CCF, Berkshire

1ST CLASP

Rank	Initials	Surname	Org	Unit
CAPT	L	DODDS	ACF	1st (Northern Ireland) Bn ACF
MAJ	A P	BARTON	ACF	1st Bn Highlanders ACF
SMI	A H W	SMYTH	ACF	1st Bn Highlanders ACF
CAPT	A J	MACIVER	ACF	1st Bn Highlanders ACF
SMI	D	MILLER	ACF	1st Bn Highlanders ACF
MAJ	A B	DURRAND	ACF	1st Bn Highlanders ACF
SMI	S E	MULLOY	ACF	2nd Bn The Highlanders ACF
MAJ	K	MASSON	ACF	2nd Bn The Highlanders ACF
CAPT	K A	CONNOR	ACF	2nd (Northern Ireland) Bn ACF
RSMI	J H	RAINEY	ACF	2nd (Northern Ireland) Bn ACF
LT COL	J A	TONNER	ACF	Argyll & Sutherland Highlanders Bn ACF
MAJ	C E M	CARDWELL	CCF	Bangor Grammar School CCF, Co Down
SSI	R D	TEKELL-MELLOR	CCF	Bedford School CCF Bedfordshire
CAPT	S J	HOARE	ACF	Buckinghamshire (The Rifles) ACF
CAPT	L J	TARGETT	ACF	Buckinghamshire (The Rifles) ACF
SMI	G C	OFFER	ACF	Cambridgeshire ACF
CAPT	S M F	McQUITTY	CCF	Cheltenham College CCF Gloucestershire
SMI	D	PRITCHARD	ACF	Cheshire ACF
SMI	B A C	DODSON	ACF	City & County of Bristol ACF
SMI	R S	RAY	ACF	Cleveland ACF
SSI	A J	COYLE	CCF	Colfe's School CCF, London
LT	A M	FEENEY	ACF	Cornwall ACF
MAJ	D A	SWINBURNE	CCF	Cranbrook School CCF Kent
LT	M D	HUTTON	ACF	Cumbria ACF
SMI	I F D	POWELL	ACF	Derbyshire ACF (Mercian)
SSI	K L	PARKER	ACF	Derbyshire ACF (Mercian)
MAJ	C S L	ADCOCK	ACF	Durham ACF
RSMI	T N	NEAL	ACF	Dyfed & Glamorgan ACF
MAJ	J L	PROTHEROE	ACF	Dyfed & Glamorgan ACF
CAPT	P D	MARTIN	CCF	Eastbourne College CCF East Sussex
MAJ	C W	SYMES	CCF	Eastbourne College CCF East Sussex
SMI	J R	TURP	ACF	Essex ACF
LT	M	COLLINS	ACF	Glasgow & Lanarkshire Bn ACF
LT	M C D	NICHOLS	CCF	Glenalmond College CCF Perthshire
MAJ	A	MASSON	ACF	Gloucestershire ACF
SSI	R A	BARTLITZ	ACF	Greater London South East Sector ACF
SMI	I D	DAWES	ACF	Greater Manchester ACF
SMI	D	O'HAGAN	ACF	Greater Manchester ACF
CAPT	E S	DAVIES	ACF	Gwent & Powys ACF
CAPT	L A	McLEOD	ACF	Gwent & Powys ACF
LT	S L	NORMAN	ACF	Hampshire & IOW ACF
MAJ	A	PHILPOTT	ACF	Hampshire & IOW ACF
SMI	J H	ROGERS	ACF	Hampshire & IOW ACF
CAPT	R E P	ROBSON	CCF	Harrow School CCF Middlesex
SSI	C J	ROSE	CCF	Heles School Devon
SMI	A D	BOWDEN	ACF	Hereford & Worcester ACF
SSI	L J G	EVANS	ACF	Hereford & Worcester ACF
SSI	J	BARR	ACF	Humberside & South Yorkshire ACF
LT	P S	MEARES	ACF	Humberside & South Yorkshire ACF
CAPT	A J	BURTON	ACF	Humberside & South Yorkshire ACF
MAJ	A	BROWN	CCF	King Edward VI School CCF Essex
LT	G	CAWLEY	CCF	King's College School CCF Wimbledon London
MAJ	S M	SHORT	CCF	King's Rochester CCF Kent
CAPT	D	DOBSON	ACF	Lancashire ACF
SMI	R J	UPTON	ACF	Lancashire ACF
SSI	D J	SMITH	ACF	Leicestershire, Northamptonshire & Rutland ACF
SMI	D E	BRADLEY	ACF	Lincolnshire ACF
CAPT	J F	RICHARDSON	ACF	Merseyside ACF
CAPT	V L	COLES	ACF	Middlesex & North West London ACF
SMI	D F	KRACKE	ACF	Middlesex & North West London ACF
MAJ	M J	CLAYTON	CCF	Morrison's Academy Crieff, Perthshire
CAPT	M T	STORDY	ACF	Norfolk ACF
CHPLN(CF3)	E A	JUMP	ACF	Norfolk ACF
CAPT	R C	MEDLER	ACF	Norfolk ACF
SI	R T	JORDAN	ACF	Norfolk ACF
SSI	J P	O'BRIEN	ACF	Norfolk ACF
SSI	D A	STARK	ACF	Northumbria ACF
CAPT	J P	TILL	CCF	Old Swinford Hospital School CCF West Midlands
SSI	J P	ROYAL	ACF	Oxfordshire (The Rifles) Bn ACF
CAPT	I M	CHRISTY	CCF	Sedbergh School CCF Cumbria
SSI	K	HENDERSON-THYNNE	CCF	Sevenoaks School CCF Kent
CAPT	S J	CUTHBERT	ACF	Shropshire ACF
SSI	S E	WILLIAMS	ACF	Somerset ACF
CAPT	S A	BETTY	ACF	Somerset ACF
LT	J G	KITCHING	ACF	Somerset ACF
SMI	L J R	HOPETON	ACF	Staffordshire & West Midlands (NS) ACF
CAPT	S J	HOWES	ACF	Staffordshire & West Midlands (NS) ACF
CAPT	R	CORTHINE	CCF	Stowe School CCF Buckinghamshire
SSI	J	COOKE	ACF	Suffolk ACF
MAJ	G W	HALDENBY	ACF	Suffolk ACF
SI	D J	LOMAS	ACF	Suffolk ACF
MAJ	H R	WATKINSON	ACF	Suffolk ACF
MAJ	J J	PRESTON	ACF	Suffolk ACF
RSMI	L G	SMITH	ACF	Suffolk ACF
SSI	L A E	UTTING	ACF	Suffolk ACF
CAPT	D	EARLE	ACF	Sussex ACF
SSI	H L	THREADGOLD	ACF	Sussex ACF
LT	P J	HORLEY	CCF	Sutton Valence School CCF, Kent
SMI	D	WESTALL	ACF	City & County of Bristol ACF
MAJ	S K	ELLEN	CCF	The Kings School Worcester
LT COL	C A	THOMPSON	CCF	Thomas Deacon Academy Cambridgeshire
MAJ	P	MAZUR	CCF	Trinity School CCF Surrey
CAPT	R E	DEEGAN	ACF	Warwickshire & West Midlands (South Sector) ACF
CAPT	C	SMITH	CCF	Wellington College CCF, Berkshire
SMI	G J	MACALISTER	ACF	West Lowland Bn ACF
SSI	T	WALLACE	ACF	West Lowland Bn ACF
SMI	G L	WAKELAM	ACF	West Lowland Bn ACF
SSI	K N	MORTIMER	ACF	Wiltshire ACF
SSI	J	WILLIAMS	ACF	Wiltshire ACF
LT COL	S	WILLIAMS	ACF	Wiltshire ACF

CADET FORCES MEDAL

SI	R A	CLARK	ACF	1st (Northern Ireland) Bn ACF
LT	S	COCHRANE	ACF	1st (Northern Ireland) Bn ACF
SMI	C J	HETHERINGTON	ACF	1st (Northern Ireland) Bn ACF
SSI	G	McFADDEN	ACF	1st (Northern Ireland) Bn ACF
SMI	S N	STEWART	ACF	1st (Northern Ireland) Bn ACF
SMI	C	FARMER	ACF	1st (Northern Ireland) Bn ACF
SSI	I	GREGOR	ACF	1st Bn The Highlanders ACF
CAPT	R A	CAMERON	ACF	1st Bn The Highlanders ACF
SMI	K	BRYANT	ACF	1st Bn The Highlanders ACF
LT	A B	DURRAND	ACF	1st Bn The Highlanders ACF
SMI	P I	FORMAN	ACF	1st Bn The Highlanders ACF
COL	S J	McCAMMOND	ACF	2nd (Northern Ireland) Bn ACF
CAPT	C I	COOPER	ACF	2nd (Northern Ireland) Bn ACF
CAPT	D G	McDOWALL	ACF	2nd (Northern Ireland) Bn ACF
SSI	W R J	McMAHON	ACF	2nd (Northern Ireland) Bn ACF
SI	C A	DEVLIN	ACF	2nd Bn The Highlanders ACF
MAJ	I M	BANYARD	ACF	Argyll & Sutherland Highlanders Bn ACF
SMI	N	EDMUNDS	ACF	Argyll & Sutherland Highlanders Bn ACF
CAPT	N A	ARCHIBALD MBE	ACF	Argyll & Sutherland Highlanders Bn ACF
SSI	D R	MARSHALLSAY	ACF	Bedfordshire & Hertfordshire ACF
CHPLN(CF3)	P F	TURNBULL	ACF	Bedfordshire & Hertfordshire ACF
COL	A J	EVERY	ACF	Bedfordshire & Hertfordshire ACF
SI	T P	EDWARDS	ACF	Bedfordshire & Hertfordshire ACF
SI	R M	BOND	ACF	Bedfordshire & Hertfordshire ACF
LT	T A	EVERETT	ACF	Bedfordshire & Hertfordshire ACF
SMI	M A	FREEMAN	ACF	Bedfordshire & Hertfordshire ACF
CAPT	T J	LAWRENCE	ACF	Bedfordshire & Hertfordshire ACF
CAPT	J G	MANGAN	ACF	Bedfordshire & Hertfordshire ACF
MAJ	S E	PRYOR	ACF	Bedfordshire & Hertfordshire ACF
CAPT	M E	AGGREY	CCF	Benenden School Kent
LT	J L	HUDSON	ACF	Buckinghamshire (The Rifles) ACF
SSI	G M	PEARMAN	ACF	Buckinghamshire (The Rifles) ACF
SMI	M A	CONNELL	ACF	Buckinghamshire (The Rifles) ACF
SSI	J D S	MURRAY	ACF	Buckinghamshire (The Rifles) ACF
LT	B A	FISHER	ACF	Buckinghamshire (The Rifles) ACF
MAJ	D T	NEWBURY	CCF	Bury Grammar Schools CCF Lancashire
CAPT	R	STEWART	ACF	Cambridgeshire ACF
MAJ	J A	GROGAN	ACF	Cambridgeshire ACF
MAJ	G R	HAMMOND	ACF	Cambridgeshire ACF
SMI	M P	GROVES	ACF	Cambridgeshire ACF
CAPT	C	ALLEN	ACF	Cambridgeshire ACF
SMI	J	PERRY	ACF	Cambridgeshire ACF
SMI	J P	GWYNNE	CCF	Cheltenham College CCF Gloucestershire
CAPT	V F	JOHNSON	ACF	Cheshire ACF
LT	P	MADDOCK	ACF	Cheshire ACF
SMI	P A	DRING	ACF	Cheshire ACF
SMI	S B	CONNOR	ACF	Cheshire ACF
2LT	C	MEDLOCK	ACF	Cheshire ACF
CAPT	D J	NIGHY	CCF	Churcher's College CCF Hampshire
2LT	W	BINDER	ACF	City of London & North East Sector ACF
SSI	R L	CROCKSON	ACF	City of London & North East Sector ACF
LT	J T	KIRK	ACF	City of London & North East Sector ACF
SMI	S	FARRAR	ACF	City of London & North East Sector ACF
LT	M	TAYLOR	ACF	City of London & North East Sector ACF
SMI	E	TAYLOR	ACF	Cleveland ACF
CAPT	I G	CRAMMOND	ACF	Cleveland ACF
SSI	S A	JONES	ACF	Clwyd & Gwynedd ACF
SI	L J	ASHTON-HUGHES	ACF	Clwyd & Gwynedd ACF
SMI	R G	JONES	ACF	Clwyd & Gwynedd ACF
CAPT	D	LANKSHEAR	ACF	Clwyd & Gwynedd ACF
CAPT	C	LLOYD	ACF	Clwyd & Gwynedd ACF
SMI	J P	GRAINGER	ACF	Cornwall ACF
LT	J J	PENGELLY	ACF	Cornwall ACF

MAJ	D A	SWINBURNE	CCF	Cranbrook School CCF Kent
SSI	A P	MARSHALL	ACF	Cumbria ACF
SSI	J H	WOOD	ACF	Derbyshire ACF
SMI	L	ROLLISSON	ACF	Derbyshire ACF
SSI	N	COOPER	ACF	Derbyshire ACF
LT	M R	DICKERSON	ACF	Derbyshire ACF
SSI	J D	WOOD	ACF	Derbyshire ACF
SSI	I M	ABRAHAM	ACF	Devon ACF
SMI	M L	DAVEY	ACF	Devon ACF
SMI	A P	SMITH	ACF	Devon ACF
CAPT	P A	ATKIN	ACF	Devon ACF
SMI	A T	DUDGEON	ACF	Devon ACF
SSI	D	POLLARD	CCF	Downside School Somerset
SMI	I	BLAND	ACF	Durham ACF
SMI	C M	TURNER	ACF	Durham ACF
CAPT	K	CRAMMOND	ACF	Durham ACF
SMI	G C	SUWINSKI	ACF	Durham ACF
2LT	L J	BROWN-SCHOFIELD	ACF	Durham ACF
CAPT	H E	LONGSTAFF	ACF	Durham ACF
LT	J T C	MILLER	ACF	Durham ACF
SSI	O D G	POWELL	ACF	Dyfed & Glamorgan ACF
MAJ	D	PRIDDY	ACF	Dyfed & Glamorgan ACF
LT	J E	GREEN	ACF	Dyfed & Glamorgan ACF
LT	V	BURFORD	CCF	Eastbourne College CCF East Sussex
CAPT	W J	TURKINGTON TD	CCF	Edinburgh Academy CCF Lothian
LT	R D B	BURGESS	CCF	Epsom College CCF Surrey
SI	R F	JONES	ACF	Essex ACF
SSI	J V	SCOTT	ACF	Essex ACF
SSI	W S	BURNS	CCF	Fettes College CCF Edinburgh
LT	M	JACK	ACF	Glasgow & Lanarkshire Bn ACF
LT	A S	McHUGH	ACF	Glasgow & Lanarkshire Bn ACF
SMI	A	PENDER	ACF	Glasgow & Lanarkshire Bn ACF
CAPT	G E	DRAPER	CCF	Glenalmond College CCF Perthshire
LT	M C D	NICHOLS	CCF	Glenalmond College CCF Perthshire
SSI	K M	MILLS	ACF	Gloucestershire ACF
SSI	S R	COOK	ACF	Gloucestershire ACF
LT	A J	SANDERSON	CCF	Godolphin School CCF Wiltshire
LT	D J	HORSMAN	ACF	Greater London South East Sector ACF
MAJ	M	BECKHAM	ACF	Greater London South East Sector ACF
SMI	R	BRADBURY	ACF	Greater London South West Sector ACF
SMI	F S	GIBBINS	ACF	Greater London South West Sector ACF
2LT	C M	SOUCH	ACF	Greater London South West Sector ACF
SMI	P	BEXLEY	ACF	Greater London South West Sector ACF
SMI	N D J	RYMILL	ACF	Greater London South West Sector ACF
SSI	D	CALLAGHAN	ACF	Greater Manchester ACF
SSI	C	GRAHAM	ACF	Greater Manchester ACF
SSI	P A	BARBER	ACF	Greater Manchester ACF
SMI	M J	HILTON	ACF	Greater Manchester ACF
SSI	C M	RICHARDSON	ACF	Greater Manchester ACF
SI	A S	ZALLMAN	ACF	Greater Manchester ACF
CAPT	M J	BATES	CCF	Gresham's School CCF Norfolk
LT	A	GROUNDS	CCF	Gresham's School CCF Norfolk
SMI	J A	FORD	ACF	Gwent & Powys ACF
SMI	P A	JONES	ACF	Gwent & Powys ACF
SSI	A J	GARDNER	ACF	Hampshire & IOW ACF
LT	S L	NORMAN	ACF	Hampshire & IOW ACF
SMI	W T	AITKEN	ACF	Hampshire & IOW ACF
LT	J	IZARD	ACF	Hampshire & IOW ACF
LT	R J	LINTOTT	ACF	Hampshire & IOW ACF
CAPT	C T	DINE	ACF	Hereford & Worcester ACF
SSI	B J	KENT	ACF	Hereford & Worcester ACF
SMI	L A	ODELL	ACF	Hereford & Worcester ACF
SSI	S J	PADMORE	ACF	Hereford & Worcester ACF
LT	J J	PRICE	ACF	Hereford & Worcester ACF

To Inspire To Achieve

SSI	A D	**ENDERBY**	ACF	Hereford & Worcester ACF
SSI	A G	**EVANS**	ACF	Hereford & Worcester ACF
SSI	S C	**WOODS**	ACF	Hereford & Worcester ACF
COL	S W	**EMERSON**	ACF	Humberside & South Yorkshire ACF
LT	P S	**MEARES**	ACF	Humberside & South Yorkshire ACF
LT	N J	**LOCKYER**	ACF	Humberside & South Yorkshire ACF
CAPT	C A	**WERNHAM**	ACF	Isle of Man ACF
SMI	W	**ALLAN**	ACF	Kent ACF
LT	L A	**BOWES**	ACF	Kent ACF
LT	A S	**GRAY**	CCF	Kimbolton School CCF Cambridgeshire
CAPT	T M	**LLOYD**	CCF	Kimbolton School CCF Cambridgeshire
SI	A J	**WALKER**	CCF	King Edward VI Grammar School CCF Lincolnshire
CAPT	B W	**KIRKHAM**	CCF	King William College, IOM
LT	S J	**BRADLEY**	CCF	King's College School CCF Wimbledon London
CAPT	J M	**STANLEY**	CCF	King's College School CCF Wimbledon London
CAPT	S J	**SHAW**	CCF	King's College Taunton Somerset
CAPT	D R J	**UNTHANK**	CCF	King's Rochester CCF Kent
SMI	A D	**DUBRAWSKI**	ACF	Lancashire ACF
COL	N D	**JURD**	ACF	Lancashire ACF
SMI	M A	**GRIMES**	ACF	Leicestershire, Northamptonshire & Rutland ACF
SMI	J A	**SILVEY**	ACF	Leicestershire, Northamptonshire & Rutland ACF
LT	C G C	**DENTON**	ACF	Leicestershire, Northamptonshire & Rutland ACF
CAPT	R J H	**GOODBAND**	ACF	Leicestershire, Northamptonshire & Rutland ACF
SI	L E	**KEIGHTLEY**	ACF	Leicestershire, Northamptonshire & Rutland ACF
SMI	S L	**SINGLETON**	ACF	Leicestershire, Northamptonshire & Rutland ACF
SSI	N	**BOYALL**	ACF	Lincolnshire ACF
COL	I M	**SACKREE**	ACF	Lincolnshire ACF
SMI	R A	**THORNE**	ACF	Lincolnshire ACF
SSI	C P J	**GUYMER**	ACF	Lincolnshire ACF
CAPT	P A	**WATSON**	ACF	Lincolnshire ACF
MAJ	P	**HOPKINS**	ACF	Lincolnshire ACF
CAPT	J M	**McKINNON**	CCF	Lord Wandsworth College Hampshire
LT	A	**MALARKY**	ACF	Lothian & Borders Bn ACF
SMI	L M	**McCAULEY**	ACF	Lothian & Borders Bn ACF
SSI	L	**MILLAR**	ACF	Lothian & Borders Bn ACF
SSI	L	**MILLAR**	ACF	Lothian & Borders Bn ACF
SSI	G	**ROY**	ACF	Lothian & Borders Bn ACF
LT	H R	**PARKER**	CCF	Merchant Taylors' School CCF, Merseyside
SSI	N	**AUSTIN**	ACF	Middlesex & North West London ACF
LT	S E	**JACKSON-LYALL**	ACF	Middlesex & North West London ACF
2LT	A A	**WEST**	ACF	Middlesex & North West London ACF
CAPT	A J	**WHITE**	CCF	Monmouth School CCF Monmouthshire
SMI	C A	**JEWELL**	ACF	Norfolk ACF
LT	M J	**ABBS**	ACF	Norfolk ACF
SSI	M A	**BISHOP**	ACF	Norfolk ACF
CHPLN(CF3)	E A	**JUMP**	ACF	Norfolk ACF
MAJ	J P S	**STOPFORD-PICKERING**	ACF	Norfolk ACF
LT	K M	**HANNANT**	ACF	Norfolk ACF
RSMI	C B	**COCKSEDGE**	ACF	Norfolk ACF
LT	M A	**HANNANT**	ACF	Norfolk ACF
SSI	J G	**PETERS**	ACF	Northumbria ACF
LT	J D	**VAN OPPEN**	ACF	Nottinghamshire ACF
SSI	A P	**DINSDALE**	ACF	Nottinghamshire ACF
SSI	M J	**EDGE**	ACF	Nottinghamshire ACF
LT	L J	**NORMAN**	ACF	Nottinghamshire ACF
SMI	C C	**RIGBY**	ACF	Nottinghamshire ACF
CAPT	R J	**ETHERINGTON**	ACF	Nottinghamshire ACF
CAPT	D G	**WRIGHT**	CCF	Oakham School CCF Rutland
MAJ	M	**THOMPSON**	CCF	Old Swinford Hospital School CCF West Midlands
SSI	K A S	**GRIGNON**	ACF	Oxfordshire (The Rifles) Bn ACF
SSI	S C	**MORGAN**	ACF	Oxfordshire (The Rifles) Bn ACF
SMI	P J	**NEAL**	ACF	Oxfordshire (The Rifles) Bn ACF
MAJ	A D	**FERGUSON**	ACF	Oxfordshire (The Rifles) Bn ACF
SMI	G E	**CLEMENTS**	ACF	Oxfordshire (The Rifles) Bn ACF
SSI	P J	**GODFREY**	ACF	Oxfordshire (The Rifles) Bn ACF
SSI	S	**WHITE**	ACF	Oxfordshire (The Rifles) Bn ACF
CAPT	J C	**WADSWORTH**	CCF	Repton School CCF Derbyshire
SI	C	**RANDALL**	ACF	Royal County of Berkshire ACF
SI	J K	**DAVIES**	ACF	Royal County of Berkshire ACF
2LT	T J	**DAY**	CCF	Rugby School CCF Warwickshire
CAPT	C R	**COOPER**	CCF	Sandbach School Cheshire
CAPT	A M	**SYKES**	CCF	Sandbach School Cheshire
CAPT	R N D	**FOLLETT**	CCF	Sedbergh School CCF Cumbria
CAPT	M N	**CAMPBELL**	ACF	Shropshire ACF
CAPT	S G	**STOKES**	CCF	Sir Roger Manwood's School CCF Kent
SSI	C J	**LANCEY**	ACF	Somerset ACF
SMI	K E	**TAYLOR**	ACF	Somerset ACF
SI	C J	**CHAPPELL**	ACF	Somerset ACF
CAPT	N W	**FONTAINE-THOMPSON**	ACF	South West London ACF
SMI	K J	**HICKS**	ACF	South West London ACF
CAPT	E B	**WALKER-BURROWS**	ACF	South West London ACF
LT COL	A J	**WOOD**	CCF	St Brigid's School CCF Denbighshire
CAPT	A R	**JONES**	CCF	St Edmund's School CCF Kent
CAPT	M A	**EASTERBROOK**	ACF	Staffordshire & West Midlands (NS) ACF
SMI	L R C	**MELLOR**	ACF	Staffordshire & West Midlands (NS) ACF
CAPT	B A	**SMITH**	ACF	Staffordshire & West Midlands (NS) ACF
SMI	D J	**WILEY**	ACF	Staffordshire & West Midlands (NS) ACF
MAJ	D	**MOODY**	ACF	Staffordshire & West Midlands (NS) ACF
CAPT	R	**CORTHINE**	CCF	Stowe School CCF Buckinghamshire
MAJ	J S	**DE GALE**	CCF	Stowe School CCF Buckinghamshire
SI	B	**CHANTRY**	ACF	Suffolk ACF
SMI	C A	**CLARKE**	ACF	Suffolk ACF
SSI	M J	**HAYES**	ACF	Suffolk ACF
SMI	A R	**HAYNES**	ACF	Suffolk ACF
SMI	Y M	**SMITH**	ACF	Suffolk ACF
SMI	A S	**DOYLE**	ACF	Suffolk ACF
SSI	T	**JEMISON**	ACF	Suffolk ACF
SSI	H J	**McCAULLY**	ACF	Surrey ACF
MAJ	D J	**WATSON**	ACF	Sussex ACF
SMI	R S	**TOMPKIN**	ACF	Sussex ACF
SMI	S	**DIGBY-CLARKE**	ACF	Sussex ACF
SSI	S R	**SAWYER**	ACF	Sussex ACF
LT	A	**PHILPOTT**	ACF	Sussex ACF
MAJ	D	**TEBAY**	ACF	Sussex ACF
CAPT	D A	**SANDERS TD**	ACF	Sussex ACF
MAJ	P	**ALE MVO**	CCF	Sutton Valence School CCF, Kent
LT	M A	**HALLERON**	CCF	Sutton Valence School CCF, Kent
CAPT	S J	**HEAD**	CCF	Sutton Valence School CCF, Kent
LT	D R L	**SAMSON**	CCF	Sutton Valence School CCF, Kent
SMI	S J	**BRYSON**	ACF	The Black Watch Bn ACF
SMI	F	**SIMPSON**	ACF	The Black Watch Bn ACF
2LT	S	**FOY**	CCF	The Blessed John Henry Newman RC College CCF Lancashire
MAJ	A W	**MATHEWSON**	CCF	The Glasgow Academy CCF, Glasgow
LT	H R	**ROBERTS**	ACF	Warwickshire & West Midlands (South Sector) ACF
SI	R C	**BENSON**	ACF	Warwickshire & West Midlands (South Sector) ACF
SI	R J	**KILBANE**	ACF	Warwickshire & West Midlands (South Sector) ACF
SSI	A R	**KELLY**	CCF	Welbeck Defence Sixth Form College Leicestershire
MAJ	C A	**HART**	CCF	Wellington College CCF, Berkshire
SSI	J	**MURPHY**	ACF	West Lowland Bn ACF
SMI	M M	**COOK**	ACF	West Lowland Bn ACF
SSI	C	**MOFFAT**	ACF	West Lowland Bn ACF
RSMI	G J	**MURRAY**	ACF	West Lowland Bn ACF
CAPT	L	**HACKETT**	ACF	Wiltshire ACF
CAPT	R J	**CRAWFORD**	ACF	Wiltshire ACF
SI	J M	**OSBEN**	ACF	Wiltshire ACF

CONSTITUTIONAL AND ADMINISTRATIVE LAW AND EU LAW

CONSTITUTIONAL AND ADMINISTRATIVE LAW AND EU LAW
SECOND EDITION

Trevor Tayleur

Second edition published 2022 by
The University of Law,
2 Bunhill Row
London EC1Y 8HQ

First edition published 2021

British Library Cataloguing in Publication Data

A catalogue record for this book is available from the British Library.

ISBN 978 1 915698 05 6

Preface

This book is part of a series of Study Manuals that have been specially designed to support the reader to achieve the SQE1 Assessment Specification in relation to Functioning Legal Knowledge. Each Study Manual aims to provide the reader with a solid knowledge and understanding of fundamental legal principles and rules, including how those principles and rules might be applied in practice.

This Study Manual covers the Solicitors Regulation Authority's syllabus for the SQE1 assessment for Constitutional and Administrative Law and EU Law in a concise and tightly focused manner. The Manual provides a clear statement of relevant legal rules and a well-defined road map through examinable law and practice. The Manual aims to bring the law and practice to life through the use of example scenarios based on realistic client-based problems and allows the reader to test their knowledge and understanding through single best answer questions that have been modelled on the SRA's sample assessment questions.

For those readers who are students at the University of Law, the Study Manual is used alongside other learning resources and the University's assessment bank to best prepare students not only for the SQE1 assessments, but also for a future life in professional legal practice.

We hope that you find the Study Manual supportive of your preparation for SQE1 and we wish you every success.

The legal principles and rules contained within this Manual are stated as at 1 June 2022.

Author acknowledgments

Trevor would like to thank Savvas Michael for reviewing and commenting on the content of chapters and sample questions and Nancy Duffield and Gary Atkinson for their source materials; their input was invaluable. Thanks must also go to David Stott for his editorial support and guidance.